The Most Excellent

Adventures of *Tenacity*

Big Waves, Cheap Wine & Farting Camels

by Cindy Fletcher-Holden

The author may be reached at fletcherart.net

Second edition.

ISBN-13: 978-1502709400

ISBN-10: 1502709406

This book is dedicated to my wonderful husband and captain, Robert.

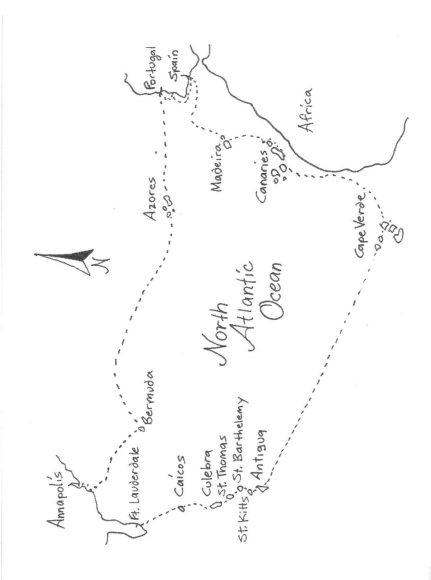

What people are saying...

Middle Of The Ocean Gazette *"Of all the tales of ocean crossing adventures, this is one of them!"*

Jackie Fletcher *"....Gripping!....."*

Dennis Biby *"Great cover! Nice to see you fixed all the mistakes."*

Cindy's Aunt Edith *"I want one."*

Somebody at the gym *"It's actually interesting!"*

Prologue

You've heard the phrases, "Life is short" or "Just do it" or "You only live once". We've heard them too. And we acted on them to bring our much talked about dream to life which was to sail across the ocean, and back.

They say that 99% of luck is planning and while that may be true, I still feel we were lucky that things fell into place. We were able to take time off from working. We had good health and support from friends and family. And we had a good boat and good crew.

I am grateful that we did go. It is very very easy not to. We have met many people who are still talking, decades later, about one day sailing somewhere. They may be waiting for retirement or waiting until they have enough money. Whichever the reason, many people talk about going and then don't. We went before retirement. We did it on a shoestring budget. If we had waited until we had plenty of money, we'd still be waiting!

Once we were into our trip, I realized that we loved places that are not universally loved. We enjoyed the places that aren't "famous". We discovered that the beauty of some of these spots come from how we viewed them. We didn't go into the Med, we didn't go to Paris. We spent months on an island with barely a few trees! But we cherished every moment. And we found even the messiest boatyard a place of beauty. And we loved the people we met.

This book is the story of our big adventure and how we did it. We are not rich folks, but we certainly feel richer now. I wanted to share the tale and hope you enjoy the ride.

CHAPTER 1

The Gale

It was a dark and stormy night. Seriously, it really was a dark and stormy night! We were on a 47' sailboat about 60 miles off the coast of Virginia in the Atlantic Ocean sailing in gale force winds. Enormous electric fingers of forked lightning protruded down from the sky, and earsplitting thunder vibrated through our bones with every explosion. Humongous waves, some as tall as houses, marched by. The sea was a wet black rocky mountain range. We were in the valleys looking up the sides of angry water, and we were on top of the waves, like on a black diamond ski slope, about to drop down into a trough like a toy boat in a turbulent tub. This lasted all night long. Our boat named *Tenacity* plowed through the thrashing seas like a battleship on a mission, carrying in it a crew of four hearty sailors bound for Europe.

It was our first night out. The day had been hot, sunny and calm. All the sails were up. We sailed along, heading out into the Atlantic, slow and steady. As I was cleaning up the galley after dinner, Robert leaned down into the companionway and announced that it was breezing up and I should make sure stuff was put away. Not a problem.

The wind kept building, and the waves, that were also building, had no order, or predictable direction, making the seas like a washing machine. We were just outside of the Chesapeake Bay, off Cape Henry, a spot notorious for sloppy weather. There are enough shoals off Cape Henry to cause steep pointy waves, in the same shape as Hershey Kisses. These waves were close together, making our ride rough and very bumpy.

We took the main sail down and reefed the jib and mizzen. The wind had built from a pleasant 10 knots, to a solid 20, and steadily increased through the 30s and 40s and gusted well into the 50s. We estimated the waves were over 20 feet high. The skies grew darker and darker. Thunder growled. Those long fingers of lightning appeared, dancing all over the horizon. Our world grew black, loud and rough. The boat rode up and then crashed down, rolling side to side. Many waves crashed over the deck. Night was upon us.

I sat heavily in the corner of the cockpit, holding onto the companionway bulkhead and for whatever reason just stared down into the cabin. And, yes, I was scared. After about an hour, nothing changed, except the time on the clock. Robert and our crew John were working as a team, Robert steering, John reading out loud the wind speed that he could see on the meter. It probably was just something for John to do since the wind was going to do what it was going to do. Hearing John read off the numbers (45, 52, 47, 58....) had a calming effect. It was pitch dark, except for the lightning that sometimes lit up the whole boat! We forged along through sloshing and wild waves. Our other crew, Bob, was safe and asleep. After a few of hours of crouching in my cockpit corner, I realized I wasn't actually doing anything to help. I excused myself and crawled into my bunk, joined by one of our cats, Perkins, who curled up next to me and purred. I slept.

When I woke, Robert was once again steering, and the winds had calmed to a more gentle 12 – 15 knots. The storm was history. It was a beautiful morning. The sun was just coming over the horizon. Robert, John and Bob were in the cockpit while I made coffee. There were dolphins playing, birds singing, butterflies fluttering. OK, there were no birds and no butterflies, but dolphins did join us to say welcome to a beautiful day. We squealed like children and clapped with delight watching the dolphins play, leap and spin through the water. They are so much fun to watch.

Nothing, nothing in the boat was broken, or had even fallen over. This was the only time in all my years of sailing that I missed my night watch. Robert and John were in complete control, and let Bob and me "off." I look back and wish I had come out for more of the storm. It was a classic ugly offshore thunderstorm with gale force winds that lasted all night. I've experienced similar, even worse weather before, but on other peoples' boats. It's different when it's your own boat. After this stormy night, I fell more in love with our boat! Not to mention Robert and his stoic sailing. It was as if we were in a movie, and the story was already written and included this big storm the first night to give us confidence in the boat. The director had highly recommended encountering this kind of weather early on an Atlantic crossing. It was a good start to this movie. By mid morning, I was more excited than ever to cross this ocean.

CHAPTER 2

The Dream

Many years before this bumpy gale, my husband Robert and I had dreamed of crossing an ocean. Not on a cruise ship, or as a passenger on another boat, but on a boat of our own. Both of us had been inspired by many other sailors, and we had already done quite of bit of offshore sailing. We didn't want to sail around the world, or cruise indefinitely. We just wanted to accomplish crossing an ocean, and to sail somewhere really cool. I grew up with boats in my family, and while still in high school, I bought a partially sunk and damaged 1939 wooden yawl that was already named *Tenacity*, (I had to look up the meaning of the word), and with the help of my dad, I rebuilt it. I managed to take this old boat down the Intracoastal Waterway and back. I also managed to crew on several offshore deliveries. So I knew I liked the ocean.

Robert, who has been sailing since he was a kid, and some of that professionally and competitively, had the opportunity to crew on a Cheoy Lee 48 ketch to the Med, stopping in the Azores, when he was 21, and he vowed to sail again to the Azores, only on his own boat. When we married, 23 years before our Atlantic adventure, I still had the original wooden *Tenacity*. We talked right away about upgrading to a bigger and more seaworthy boat, and sailing "somewhere." We were living in an apartment, I was renting a painting studio for my freelance artist work, and we were renting a boat slip. This all meant writing lots of monthly rent checks. So we ditched the apartment, moved aboard the old wood boat, and started to save money for the ocean worthy boat.

CHAPTER 3

The Boat

Several years later, we discovered the current *Tenacity* in the classified section of a local sailing magazine in 2001. We loved the word tenacity and just could not think of a better name for a boat that belonged to us. It was winter, and work was slow. We decided to take a drive to the yacht broker's office to look at this boat that seemed so intriguing on paper. The magazine ad read: "Dillon 47 Offshore Ketch, excellent for passage making..." and so on. As soon as we saw this Dillon 47, we fell in love with it! It is a semi custom fiberglass ketch based on a Bruce Robert's design. A guy named Dillon bought the plans, changed them a bit on paper and had a few boats professionally built. We didn't think it was prudent to buy the first boat we looked at, on impulse, so we shopped intensely for the next six months, and finally realized this Dillon ketch was the one after all. So, we bought it. Fortunately we also had a buyer for our old boat right away, a very good thing because we didn't want to be stuck with two boats. Soon after all the buying and selling, we began an extensive upgrade. Completing all of this would prove to take years while we continued to work, live life, and pay for each improvement.

There was a lot of work to be done. We threw out an old upright refrigerator, replaced it with a top loading custom built freezer/refrigerator box with thick insulation. We rewired the whole boat, had the engine hauled out and rebuilt, made mast step reinforcements, stripped the wood and applied new varnish inside, painted the decks, upgraded equipment, and more. All the while, we maintained our jobs, enjoyed our friends, built up my art business, and continued to advance in our beloved sport of ice dancing. For quite some time, we were in no hurry to go anywhere. Working on the boat became part of our normal routine. Life was good. We were both making money. We were getting quite good at skating, even won some competitions. We were surrounded by great friends. Who would want to leave?

Our complacency began to change in 2008 when we decided to address the rigging. We were hoping that the rig would just need repainting and a few new fittings on the boom. But on inspection, there were too many signs of age and damage. We would need everything removed, masts, booms, all the standing rigging, lifelines (we found all kinds of rust under the plastic coating) and stern and bow pulpits. The rigger went over all the work that would be needed to make our boat seaworthy for a 10,000 +mile trip. The cost could exceed $40,000. (This was with a "family" discount due to the fact that the rigger was an old friend). This was a crucial moment. We were not going to have all this work done to just go on weekend trips around the Bay. We realized that to leave the rig "as is" would not be safe for crossing an ocean. The moment we signed the work order we realized we were committed. The trip would happen! Time to be serious! We started the labor intensive and highly expensive task of replacing everything, every fitting, screw, winch, everything but the actual mast tubing, from the deck up. I jumped in and did all the sanding and prep for new paint. (My kind of work). We beefed up the thickness and weight of the stays and life lines and got larger winches. All the more appropriate for offshore sailing than what the boat had. Also, the old mast head was cracked, and it would be a short matter of time before it failed. Finally, the new, improved rig was replaced in 2010. Many thanks go out to John Callewaert , our most excellent rigger! We know how to pick the best.

CHAPTER 4

The Place

Next we got serious about the destination. We already decided on Europe by way of the Azores. We talked about going into the Med, but were not completely sold on going in. There was much political instability in North Africa, which we knew was affordable. We had wanted to go there, but now it had become possibly dangerous and our insurance company said we would not be covered if we went there. We knew that Spain and France inside the Med were very expensive, and that to head all the way to Greece and Turkey could mean more time than we could afford. We checked out France, England, and northern Europe, and after much research, talking to many other sailors, hordes of other travelers, we finally decided on Portugal as our main destination. The decision to look more into Portugal was prompted by two things. One was the possibility of having to fly a crew back to the U.S. Flights from Lisbon were much less expensive than from other major European airports. The second was strong encouragement from our rigger John to stop and explore the little towns along the Portugal coast.

The more we read and learned, the more we became intrigued with Portugal. We could also visit some of Spain, and then return by way of the Atlantic Islands that include Madeira, the Canaries, and the Caribbean islands. Now it was time to pick a date.

According to the logs kept by centuries of ocean bound sailors, the best time to cross the Atlantic heading east is May through July. We were aiming for early June. The best time to cross back west is during the trade winds, which start in November, fill in in December, and blow through February, maybe into early spring. This meant we could cross over in the spring, and return in the fall. But with all the money and energy we had put into this adventure,

15

we couldn't justify planning on heading back west the same year as going over. So we planned on wintering over in Portugal, somewhere, and then crossing back west the next year. Total time away, two years. We knew we couldn't afford more than two years with no income, so this became our plan.

Robert left his job on April 15, 2011. He then worked full time to prepare the boat, making all new sails, a new dodger, installing new instruments, solar panels and other offshore gadgets. I kept working as long as I had work, but also continued to work out the land logistics for our expected time away. I made arrangements for money matters to be handled and for the business phone to remain active (with an outgoing message that said we were on a sailing adventure). I had our address changed to a P.O box. I sublet my art studio space, finalized the crew, and started packing.

As we got into May, we got even busier and our days grew long and hectic. One large lettering job that I was trying to complete involved having some of my art digitized and printed onto vinyl. I called a good friend, John Prehn, who owns a large successful sign shop and has been helping me out for 20 years whenever I need to digitize work. I am still a purist. I specialize in hand lettering. John had long before "crossed over to the dark side" (his words), the phrase often used when a sign painter turns to computer cut vinyl lettering. When he asked why I needed my art digitized, I explained that the customer was afraid of graffiti, and I would not be around to repair my work. Vinyl could be replaced if it got vandalized. John asked why I wouldn't be around. I told him we were sailing to Portugal, to which I added "Wanna go?" I was kidding, but not entirely. I knew John had a lot of ocean experience as a Merchant Marine and also had done many sailing trips himself. So instinct must have been partly why I said "Wanna go?" The next day, he called and said he thought about it, and that he would love to join us!! Wow!! And his sign shop could continue on while he was away!

John and Robert met for the first time and bonded like brothers, (they even dress alike) and John jumped in with both feet helping to do a lot of the final preparations to the boat. We were also joined by two young guys who were looking for adventure. They did not get past Virginia however, due to unforeseen personality clashes and logistical issues. But John would prove to be a crew that helped make our voyage such a delightful one, and he became a closer friend as well.

CHAPTER 5

Sad News

In the last week of May, we received bad news. Robert's dad passed away, and on the very same day, one of our best friends, Tim Ellis, a sailor and adventurer, died in an accident. We knew that Robert's dad was not doing well in his old age, but we had hoped he would be alive long enough to follow our adventure. Tim's death was way premature. Robert took a break from boat preparations and flew to Florida to be with his family and speak at his dad's service. I became quite involved in Tim's arrangements. I mention this because of a person who was Tim's closest friend, and is one of our very best friends, Casey Brokenshire, a U.S. Diplomat, who was stationed in Iraq at the time of Tim's accident.

Casey had been instrumental to our plan. Casey had had quite of bit of sailing adventures on his 24' Bristol, with Tim as crew. Before Casey became a diplomat, he and Tim sailed that little boat to South America and back, twice! He still tells amazing stories about their adventures. He knows many people who talk about sailing off on an adventure, and then never do, for too many reasons to even try to recall. But he did it and never regrets all the miles and mishaps he had during his trips.

In 2008, Robert and I went to Africa to visit Casey and his family. He was stationed in Guinea at that time. He knew we had our boat, and he knew that we had talked about going somewhere. But he feared that we would become another casualty in the world of sailing dreams. He made Robert and me stand in front of him, hold our right hands up, and pledge: "We, Robert and Cindy Holden, promise that we will untie the lines and leave the dock, and take *Tenacity* across the ocean. We will not continue to chat about going 'some day.' We will go. We will not back out. We will go."

Best pledge we ever made next to our marriage vows! And as soon as we returned from Africa, we started on the rig, and signed that work order.

But at this time in late May of 2011, there was grieving. I needed to help Casey ensure our friend Tim had a proper send off. Casey was far away, and Tim's mom had very little money, so I acted as Casey's proxy to handle Tim's affairs. We held a service in a church that included a 5 page eulogy written by Casey, and read by me. We had a gathering of friends on our boat to spread Tim's ashes and to tell stories. We had a boatyard wake. At the wake we served National Bohemian, Tim's favorite beer. Amazingly, there was a lot of left over beer and we stowed it in our boat for later consumption. OK, you're probably wondering what this has to do with the story, but there is a point to all this. You will see. The leftover cans of Natty Boh beer become weirdly significant later.

CHAPTER 6

Failing Fittings

Still sad, we got back to working on the boat. One of our many new acquisitions was a watermaker. Since we were busy with so much stuff, we talked about waiting to install it later, while going down the Bay or even offshore on a calm day. Our boat holds 550 gallons of water. But we bought a watermaker anyway, thinking that with one we'd always have plenty of water for showers, and would have good water in case we went to a place that had bad water. After a while, we decided that we should not install it ourselves. We hired a professional. That professional was Ricardo, who knows his way around watermakers.

As Ricardo was installing the plumbing that brings the water in from the outside, he pushed the hose onto a bronze through hull fitting. "Through hull fittings" are hollow plugs, installed into the hull of boats. They can be opened and closed with a valve to allow water to come in on purpose. They have been made out of metals like bronze, and are now more commonly made out of thick plastics. We had many of our through hull fittings replaced during a haul out a few years before this, but this particular one, made out of bronze, seemed fine and even passed a recent survey. But now, as Ricardo pushed the hose onto it, the fitting disintegrated! Water flowed into our boat! Not a good thing! This was not how we wanted to make water! Ricardo took off his sock and shoved it into the hole. The flow slowed.

Miraculously, Robert showed up and grabbed a foam form fitting plug and jammed it into the gushing hole and stopped the water. Then he and Ricardo immediately moved the boat to a boatyard a block away from our marina and we hauled out. Good thing we didn't try this task offshore. There had been no way for the surveyor to detect the bronze in the fitting to be corroding from the inside out. One theory is that it had been tightened too much when it was originally put in, back more than 20 years before, and cracked a tiny bit. Water may have been seeping into the bronze for enough time to turn it into crumbles. So, now, during this unexpected haul out, we replaced every through hull fitting that was older than two years.

Blog: Getting Ready to Go

May 23 2011
38:97.29N 76:50.12W

Our position is still Annapolis. The departure date is mid June. Some say the boat will never be ready and perhaps they are right. We will leave nonetheless. We may leave with some new things still in a box but the boat will be ready to sail and sail well. Today we ordered a new traveler from the rigger who is doing our new inner forestay. He knows our schedule and can make it work. I am almost done packing my studio of 8 years. A monumental task in itself. And as you see, I am learning how to use this web diary/sail blog.

CHAPTER 7

Down To The Wire

Several days later, the through hull fitting job accomplished, we were back at our marina and heading into the homestretch! Robert made the dodger, a canvas "windshield" that gave our cockpit a wonderful, cozy, shaded and protected place to be during wet or windy weather. It was a tough fit, but Robert made it work, bending, cutting, fitting, and installing the heavy duty stainless steel frame and perfectly fitted canvas. It was beautiful. Then we installed a new main traveler, a strip of flat black aluminum track that takes up the entire width of the boat, allowing us to trim the position of the main sail and boom. It was installed right in front of the dodger, (lots of tight measurements) and looked spectacular, making our old boat look more like a racing machine. This new traveler replaced an old one that was basically useless because it was so short. During all this, I took apart and cleaned and greased the cockpit winches. John reinforced our deck's locker hatches, and I went to work inside the cabin.

Blog: Final Countdown

June 17 2011
38:97.29N 76:50.12W

We are shooting for Sunday, (Father's Day) or very early Monday. The Monday forecast is pretty sweet. Robert is still building our new dodger. I cleaned and greased the cockpit winches today. They had to be taken apart to receive new strippers. Yes, we'll have strippers on the boat!

We just had a huge new main sheet traveler installed. It looks like the boat is all grown up now!

The cabin is filled with lots of tools, spare parts, cups of screws, padeyes, nuts, barrel bolts, inch worms, cabin hooks, stainless elbow fittings, wire ties, charts, cordless drills, rolls of paper towels and a year's worth of cat food, just to name some of the stuff that we are stepping over and pawing through!

Stay tuned for more prep stuff.

I bought every last stainless steel "tie down" from the hardware store (I call them inch worms, because they look like little inch worms) and I took upon the task of stowing and arranging every single loose item in the boat, all the while envisioning a knock down or roll over. I did not want things to go flying about in the cabin.

Finally I got serious about shopping for food, a chore I was saving for last I had cooked off shore before and had done deliveries that lasted up to 13 days. I knew how to provision. I made a list, but found it much more enjoyable to walk up and down the aisles, thinking about different things to prepare, picturing myself in a rocking and pitching galley. I loaded up with pasta, rice, canned meats, canned vegetables, canned fruits, canned soups, broth, milk, paper products, zip lock bags, aluminum foil, more veggies, more meat, more pasta, rice, spices, boxed milk, nuts, more nuts, baking supplies, cookies, crackers, soda, juices, more canned meats, more fruit and veggies, then sturdy vegetables like cabbage, potatoes, onions, more onions, lots of garlic, carrots, frozen veggies of all flavors, frozen meat, frozen fish, fresh meat, more fresh fruits and veggies and bread and cheese, lots of cheese. I made many trips to many stores and finally reached a point where I thought we were good. The boat was filled with provisions! Including our ice skates! What a sight. A cabin filled with bags and bags of groceries, cases of soda, beer and water, cases of paper towels and toilet paper. Tool boxes filled with tools, buckets of fishing supplies, spare parts, more hardware, books, more books, engine parts, fuel filters, oil filters, spare engine belts, more inch worms, batteries, cat food, and two pairs of ice skates. This did not look like a boat ready for a leisurely weekend sail. I continued the task of more stowing, securing stuff down, keeping notes, rearranging, changing notes, all the while the butterflies were increasing in my stomach.

At one point, I was getting cold feet. I said to John, "Why are we doing this? I have a wonderful career here, great friends, family, a good life!" John replied, "You have to do this! You will sail across the ocean. And then you will sail back. You will have an experience no one can take away. And then you'll come back, and go to some party, or some gathering, and hear the exact same stories, same news, same gossip as before you left, and you will say 'John was right'. "

Amen.

The day had arrived. It was time to leave the dock.

CHAPTER 8

Tuna Tower Trivets and Testy Tornadoes

My sister Jackie and my brother Keith were there to help with final washdown and cast off. And we did indeed cast off. It was a very significant moment, untying the lines and leaving the dock, and all of the dock's securities, the electricity, the grassy lawn at the marina, my studio two blocks away and financial income. It was time to leave all this behind and move towards a future somewhat unknown.

Scary.

We headed down the Bay into a brisk southerly wind, a bumpy uncomfortable ride, but we were off. We made it into a harbor in Little Creek, Virginia, a suburb of Norfolk, just inside the Chesapeake Bay Tunnel at the mouth of the Bay. It was 1:00 in the morning. We decided to stop for the rest of the night, and top off the fuel tank first thing in the morning before heading out into the ocean. We tied up at the fuel dock and were the first ones there when they opened in the morning. The fuel pumps there are huge and designed to pump many hundreds of gallons of fuel into "mega" motor yachts. Still, it was a total surprise to the dock attendant when she squeezed the nozzle and 50 gallons rushed out of the hose and into our tank in less than a couple of seconds. The speed and pressure of the fuel gushing into our tank, which is under our cabin's sole (floor), caused several of our fuel inspection ports to crack and, well, kind of explode, allowing fuel to slosh over the top of the tank. What a mess! We had stinky diesel all over our cabin floor and an urgent job to do. The inspection ports were made of a thick threaded plastic, and they screwed down in place. But they were old, now cracked and ruined and needed to be replaced, immediately, and preferably in aluminum. We couldn't let this slow us down!

Without wasting a minute, we pumped out the excess fuel, cleaned up the cabin floor, and went in search of a metal worker who might be able to make aluminum discs, (quickly). We needed eight of these, about seven inches in diameter, and 1/8th inch thick, with screw holes drilled around the perimeter. While Robert went to find someone, John and I prepped the surface of the tank for the bedding of the new ports. Robert found a marine welder right across the creek. The welder had started a job building a tuna tower on a sport fishing boat. But the customer had walked off the job, leaving the welder with, I am not making this up, eight aluminum discs, seven inches in diameter, 1/8th inch thick, with holes drilled for securing the plates in place! What are the odds of that happening? He said we could have the whole stack for fifty bucks. Seemed like someone was watching out for us.

Anyway, we were back in business in a matter of days. This was when our young crew members left. Too much work and too much time. Their loss. So as we were installing the new strong inspection ports, John contacted an old friend of his, Bob, to join us. Bob, excited to sail in the ocean, arrived the next day. And off we went.

We not only checked the weather with the radio, but had a professional weather router communicating with us by way of e-mail and phone. The forecast was typical summer, hazy, hot and humid with a chance of afternoon thunderstorms. The general offshore wind and Gulf Stream forecast, according to our weather router, was very favorable for leaving. We sailed along, excited to be officially in the ocean.

The director had other plans.

Not far from the Chesapeake Bay Bridge Tunnel, the horizon looked a bit "hazy." Not dark, just kind of hazier than it was earlier, and we thought a little afternoon squall might be coming and Robert went to the cabin top to take down the main sail. Right before he got to the halyard, the wind gusted and the boat spun around like a gyro toy, the boom crashing from side to side. The wind had gone from a fluky eight from the south, to 50 knots of a swirly, gusty vortex, then settled to a steady 20 out of the west, and we had no steering. It all happened really fast.

Robert went below to check the steering system, which is hydraulic, and begins at the wheel in the cockpit and follows a series of chains to a hydraulic pump located under the aft bunk. There, under the bunk, an "L" shaped, nine inch long bronze tiller, a good half inch thick, that controls the rudder under the boat, had literally snapped in two! Like a pencil! There was that much pressure in the spinning of the boat! The hydraulic system works in a way that where you have the wheel set in the cockpit, is where the rudder is set, until you move the wheel. So the boat spun, the rudder did not, and the internal bronze tiller broke. If we had cable steering, it could have caused the rudder to slam and the wheel to spin, either one causing other kinds of damage, like a broken hand. But this is something we'll never know and at that moment we needed to deal with the situation immediately.

We had an emergency tiller that we never had to use before. The way it works is it attaches manually to the top of the rudder post, which also under the aft bunk, and someone has to hand steer with this awkward tiller, while standing on the bunk frame, sticking their head out the hatch. An OK solution, but there was a problem. The shape of the base of the tiller did not fit correctly onto the rudder post, making it nearly impossible to control. Mental note, this has to be redesigned. Robert struggled the best he could while John, Bob and I navigated and watched for traffic. Another issue here is we were smack in the middle of the shipping lanes, with barely any steering. We soon realized it was a dangerous enough situation to call the Coast Guard. They came out in their 40' cutter. One of the Coast Guard guys snickered and said he could steer our boat with the emergency tiller.

"My mama didn't raise no wimp," he said. After about one minute he said "I can't figure this thing out." Told you so.

I had a moment of clarity right after the spinning and took a photo of the dramatic sky. Later that night, when we arrived back at the Little Creek dock safely with the help of the Coast Guard, and after we all opened an insanely delicious beer and made dinner, I looked the photo in my camera and noticed long fingers of black clouds spewing towards the water. We got hit by a tornado! Which, of course, explains all the spinning! Robert is convinced to this day that had we not replaced the rig, we would have lost it during this twister.

Well, now we had to not only fix the bronze tiller, we also needed to address the design of the emergency tiller. The next morning, Robert returned to our welder across the creek. He could make a new internal tiller to replace the bronze, out of stainless, but it would take a month and cost $1000. Not going to happen. So he steered Robert to a bronze worker, one of the only bronze shops left in all of Virginia, right up the road, who could fix our broken tiller in a day for $80. While that was being done, we cut down the emergency tiller, and had the first welder re-cut its shape so it would fit perfectly. Then, Robert rigged a system of blocks and line so that someone could actually sit outside and steer. Much better.

We picked up the repaired and beefed up bronze tiller. The welder said he made it stronger than when we came in, but noted it had been broken and repaired before. We made a mental note to keep an eye on it. We were once again ready to head out into the ocean.

We left the morning after all the metal work was done. We had a beautiful sunny sail out of the mouth of the Chesapeake Bay. This was finally our first true day out. At last. By that evening the gale hit. It was the official "dark and stormy night."

Blog: July 4th Light Show

July 5 2011
36:51.00N 75:43.00W

BIG Ass storm last night! 45, 50 – 60 kt winds, wildly confused seas and lightning everywhere. A very impressive light show! However, I'd rather be stuck in DC traffic listening to NPR.

Nice now. SW winds, 12- 15 and sunny. No broken steering arms today. 2 scared kitties.

CHAPTER 9

Squalls, Sun, Poignant Poetry and Pungent Potatoes

By the following morning the nasty storm was becoming a memory. It was an exquisite day after the storm and our spirits were lifted. I was ecstatic that nothing had fallen and nothing had broken. The only weird thing was a little bit more fuel appeared above the tank. We had replaced every single inspection port, and every one was secure and tight, with no sign of leaking. So where was this fuel coming from? It wasn't much, but still, even a little bit of diesel fuel on the floor can be dangerous not to mention smelly. We cleaned it up, and it seemed to be gone. We kept a watchful eye on the tank's top.

The first night after the Big Storm was beautiful. Another great meal and sunset. Dolphins came to visit! What a boost to morale dolphins can be! They smile, they jump and spin, and splash about, and they seem to thoroughly enjoy being alive. We behaved like little kids clapping and squealing with joy while watching them. They are such wonderful creatures.

Blog: Now This is What We Signed Up For

July 6 2011
36:23.00N 74:30.00W

beautiful day, awesome evening. great sunset and delicious dinner!

Big cold front coming in a few days. expecting big winds and more storms. we had a good run through the program last night. practice makes .... really bad hair days!

The next couple of days took us across the Gulf Stream, which can be nasty. And it was nasty, but after that first stormy night, *Tenacity* had proven to be strong. I trusted the boat. The waves in the Gulf Stream are often huge and close together, but also wickedly blue and beautiful, and sometimes carry sea creatures too far north, fooling them with the stream's warmth. The sailing was rough but manageable. We reefed and trimmed sails accordingly, and steered with control. Although steering was physically challenging, we were in control. There are often lots of squalls in the "Stream," which we had, but they are short lived and easy to deal with. Even with sideways rain and 40 knots of wind, we would reef and plow ahead, knowing these squalls usually last less than 30 minutes. The waves were big and seemed to have personality. We would name them. We'd say "There goes Leroy." The sun, when out, was hot and the air was sticky and humid. Having a professional sailmaker on board means our sails are always trimmed right, and the boat sails along basically without incident. I'll take monotony over danger any day. I actually enjoyed the heavy weather sailing through the Gulf Stream.

Blog: Gulf Stream

July 6 2011
36:35.00N 72:46.00W

Beautiful day yesterday. followed by beautiful evening complete with sunset. squalls all night, nothing to write home about, except I am writing about them! More squalls all day today. nice big SW wind and solid waves rolling along. Some big. Just started to rain.

May be a good time for laundry? Really bad hair days out here. Whoever invented chocolate covered espresso beans deserves a medal of some kind. they are perfect for that 2 AM watch!

Ode to Helly Hansen

a poem by Cindy

With driving rain and winds of 40 knots, how long will THIS one last? I'm askin,

thank God for Helly Hansen

"Kersplash" went the wave on my head and down my back, how many more of THESE today? I'm askin,

thank God for Helly Hansen

With panoramic skies of ugly squalls and lightning, will it ever clear? I'm askin,

thank God for Helly Hansen

Dressed from head to toe in gear made for foul weather,

Complete with offshore safety harness, stainless clip and tether,

I look these storms into their eyes and I'm askin,

Will I do this again? You bet!

But not without my Helly Hansen!

Life below was not an easy task. Even sleeping was an event. We'd be tossed up and down, sometimes airborne. John, up forward, needed to tie himself in his bunk. Robert and I could be tossed about in our bigger bunk, and our bunk is all the way in the back of the boat, so the motion is less severe than up forward.

Cooking became an extreme sport. Our galley is small which is an advantage offshore. I could brace my body in between the sink and fridge. Facing the sink and cutting board, I had my back up against the fridge and legs apart and knees ready to bend to absorb the motion. In this position, I could easily reach everything on the stove to my left and sink and cutting board in front of me. Then, if I needed to get something out of the fridge, I did a pirouette around and faced the fridge, now with my back up against the sink counter. It was like a dance. In fact, all that ice dancing acted like training! The stove is gimbaled, and we have brackets that keep pots in place but they don't work all that well. I stayed vigilant when I had hot pots on the stove, knowing that burns from hot water spilling can be very dangerous. I would put an extra hot pot in one of the deep sinks so I could have only one burner going at a time. In calm weather, I'd have more burners on but would still be a pot watcher. In really rough seas, I could still manage minimal hot meals except for two nights in the Gulf Stream, when all I could manage to serve was sliced sausage, cheese, veggies and crackers. It was actually quite good and hit the spot.

Steering also became a sport. I cherished the experience. Our auto pilot, (self steering), is electric and uses a huge amount of power. So we elected to hand steer, unless the engine was on. I would stand up on the cockpit seats, one foot on either side and the helm in front of me. The sensation felt as if I were riding two horses, one under each foot, and the horses would be running, and at any moment the horses would turn and go UP the hill and then run DOWN the hill, galloping along at full speed. What a rush. I'd never ridden two horses at once but this is how I imagined it would be! I made a mental note more than once to actually try to do this on horses. Maybe it'll happen. For a few days in the Gulf Stream it was too rough to do much other than steer, eat, and sleep. But these days did not last that long.

We noticed more fuel over the top of the tank. Not much, but enough to cause concern. Where was it coming from? We had cleaned every square inch of the tank's top when we installed the new ports. We needed to figure this out. Somewhere, we had fuel leaving the tank. We had to solve this problem. We could turn back (no!!), we could continue straight on to the Azores (good), or, we could make a stop in Bermuda, since we were already pretty much heading in that direction (yes!!).

So we adjusted our sails and steered for Bermuda a mere 400 miles away. Funny, sailing a distance of 80 miles used to seem like a long trip, but out there, that day, 400 miles sounded like just a small hop. When did my perspective get all switched?

At one point we all noticed a pungent aroma coming from somewhere in the main cabin. About a day after it was first noticed, it became too strong to ignore. I followed my nose and discovered a bag of potatoes behind a lee cloth that were rotting. Potatoes! These were supposed to be "sturdy" vegetables. And in my smell search, I realized some of the cabbage was turning bad, and quickly! I would later learn more about storing these kinds of vegetables. But at that moment these were tossed.

Robert kept searching for the source of the fuel leak. Then, about a day away from Bermuda, Robert announced "I found it!!" It was an old fuel gauge sensor, that of course never worked (we never met a single other sailing cruiser with a working fuel gauge in the whole two years. They all used dip sticks). This old nonworking fuel gauge was under the galley cabinets, which were built on top of the gauge. To see it, Robert had to get on his hands and knees, completely pull out the bottom drawer and put his head all the way in the drawer space and look down. There it was! The little sensor had been placed into a hole the size of the top of a Minute Maid frozen orange juice can. It had a pile of epoxy plopped over it. The epoxy never stuck to the fiberglass tank surface and fuel was trickling out around it. We actually pulled an orange juice can from the freezer and wondered if we could make the lid work. And I bet we could have, but we were already looking forward to seeing Bermuda and decided to have a proper one made. At least we knew the source of the fuel! It felt like winning a lottery!

CHAPTER 10

Bermuda

Once we were through the Gulf Stream the rest of the sailing to Bermuda was quite pleasant. We actually sighted the lights of the island in the night and slowed the boat down so that we would arrive in daylight. And it was a spectacular sunrise for my first international landfall! Another time zone! And a stamp in our passports that read "entry by sea." Mark Twain had said, "Bermuda is paradise, but you have to sail through purgatory to get there." I understand now.

Our visit in Bermuda was only four days. After checking in with immigration, we went to a "marina" called Captain Smokes, to find a tall solid concrete seawall to tie up to, no office, but a freestanding bath house and little grassy yard. It was wonderful. We also met Neil and Laurie who had arrived earlier on a 28' Triton. We instantly bonded with them and swapped Gulf Stream tales.

After a few chores, like washing our foul weather gear and getting laundry together, we needed to find a welder to make our new fuel gauge hole cover. About a mile from the "marina" we found Leroy, the welder, a tattooed, chain wearing, nose studded Samuel Jackson look-alike that could have been plucked from central casting. We walked into his impressive shop wielding our juice can lid and a hole diagram. Leroy had us fixed up by the next morning.

We were in the town of St. Georges. Its economy relies heavily on cruise ships. On the second morning I went for a run and ran right by the landing where the cruise ships tie up. THRONGS of tourists were getting off, all dressed in floppy hats, sparkly flip flops, oversized sunglasses, bright sundresses or long shorts and tank tops, carrying huge purses and tiny cameras. They all moved as one, in the same direction, same speed, same expression. I was going the opposite way. I suddenly felt like a lemming who didn't get the lemming memo, or who refused to follow the pack. I felt oddly invisible.

I quickly discovered the best time to go to the grocery store was after 6:00 p.m. when the cruise ships have already departed. I understand that the locals love the cruise ships because the passengers spend money. But we found that the atmosphere in town was more laid back and friendly after 6:00. The streets were far less crowded. We were treated with a lot of respect. The locals knew what we had gone through to arrive in a small boat.

We loved Bermuda but we had an ocean to cross. Crew Bob did not enjoy his Storm/Gulf Stream experience and decided to go home. He blamed his age (71), and I must say here he was a good crew and steered well. But it was his decision. We later met many sailors well into their 70s who were strong and able, crossing oceans and making passages. It was Bob's comfort zone and his choice. We couldn't force him to stay, so we bid farewell. This left just us three. But that was OK. We got a good night's rest and planned to head out early the next morning of July 16, 12 days since we left the US coast. It was time to point the boat east and head out into the ocean.

Blog: The Trackless Sea By John Prehn

July 21, 2011

Bermuda sinks quickly below the horizon, a mid-Atlantic Brigadoon, leaving us alone on the torn blue circle

Of the ocean. Sun and clouds, waves with whitecaps in their endless patterns. Only a few birds notice our passage.

The sea seems so vast, anonymous, trackless.

But we know exactly where we are. Half a dozen wonderfully compact devices constantly update with our precise location.

I think they can tell which side of the boat I'm sitting on. With our widgets and their waypoints, we chart our path north

and east, seeking out favorable winds and current.

Others have passed this way. Days, years, centuries ago. Seeking what? Exploration, adventure, commerce;

They all had their reasons. And each of them subject to this endless circle of sea and sky. As are we. Seeking what?

Well, the Azores, for one thing. ("Why don't you just fly there?") But there is more, somewhere in this trackless blue

horizon.

CHAPTER 11

Falling In Love With The Ocean

The morning of the 16th was crisp and clear. A cold front had blown through and the winds were still northeasterly at about 20 knots. We were beating across the Atlantic (is that allowed?) but the boat's sails were trimmed to perfection. *Tenacity* sailed so steady that we barely had to touch the wheel. The waves were quite manageable, not too big and far apart from each other. *Tenacity* was in her glory, sailing herself.

The night was clear and breathtaking. The moon was so bright it cast shadows on the deck. We still didn't have to touch the wheel. I loved my midnight watch, under the gazillion stars, so good to be alive out there.

Since we were down to three people, we held three hour watches, giving us six hours off. This proved quite perfect. We didn't have the same watch schedule every day, and six hours was plenty of time to sleep. Holding watch and steering for 3 hours was not too bad. Of course, those last 30 minutes during a night watch were hard, but we had lots of help from our chocolate covered coffee beans and wasabi trail mix.

Fitness has been a part of my life for a very long time. I actually worried about being offshore so long without being able to run. Before we left I worked with a trainer and came up with a variety of workout routines that I could do in the cabin. I would just need to be disciplined. I was talking to a friend about this one day. He said, "Oh, just buy your self a portable elliptical."??? I searched on line and found a mini elliptical for only $70 and ordered it. It was small enough to fit in the corner of the main cabin, on the floor, by the main mast compression post and be out of the way. It doesn't have the arm rails like the ones in gyms. It's perfect. When I used it, I pulled it out and set it facing our new grab rail. There I could workout with the elliptical while holding on to the rail and read a book. This took way less discipline than doing all the moves I had learned, which meant I had no excuse to not do it every day for 45 minutes. It was enough cardio to work up a sweat. After Bermuda, I got into a regular routine. Along with the elliptical, I incorporated all kinds of workout routines in the cabin and out in the cockpit. Steering was physical, as was just moving around, but only when it was windy. I wanted to know I was able to get a regular workout even in calm conditions.

Blog: Offshore Gym

July 19 2011

37:34.00N 61:59.00W

I am (was) an avid member of a gym called the Annapolis Athletic Club. I think I should open our own gym called the North Atlantic Athletic Club. While not as nice as AAC, we do have some unique qualities. While we can't offer individual TV monitors with unlimited cable, we do offer a brightly lit GPS screen giving thrilling accounts on where you've been and where you're going in bright blue and pink. And while we can't offer clean hot showers, we do offer constantly moving (a workout in itself) trickle showers that compel you to brag about how little water you've used ("I just used a Tea Cup") And while we don't have freshly laundered towels, we do have the Deluxe Ever Damp Towel system, one per person in bright designer colors.

AND we offer the recently patented exclusive King Neptune Ocean Spray Salt and Sun Skin Care system, keeping your skin damp and clammy, along with the King Neptune Ocean Spray Salt and Wind Hair Care System, always sure to frizz even the silkiest hair!

We are not able to offer free classes like Pilates or Yoga, but we'll give you a compass course and a wheel to steer and 3 hours to do it! Get strong core muscles in just days!! Sign up now!

A boat, or ship, on the ocean is like its own little planet. While one would think it would be claustrophobic to be on a small boat for so many days, the expanse of the ocean in every direction zeroes that out. We were quite independent out there. We had all the electric conveniences you need. Some things we decided to live without, such as the electric coffee pot that uses over 50 amps (a lot of juice) so we wrapped it up and stowed it away. Instead, we heated water and poured it over fresh ground beans through a filter. Perfect! We decided not to have a microwave, another electric hog. We would turn on things like hair driers, vacuums, and battery chargers only when the engine was running. Even when we had plenty of wind, we'd run the engine one hour a day, and that topped off the battery bank. We had lights, music, water pressure (electric pump), a refrigerator, freezer and instruments. These all use little power. Some of the crew even watched movies on their computers. I preferred books, but the movie option was there.

One of the nicest frills we had, thanks to technology, was a satellite phone e-mail service. With this we could stay in touch with Bob, the weather router located in Florida, and our friends and family back home. I would type away on the computer, sometimes sitting on the cabin floor if it was bumpy, and then plug the phone into the computer. Then I'd turn on the phone and hold it up towards a hatch so the antenna would be exposed to open air. It would dial, register, connect, send and receive e-mail, bing bang done! Just like that! Then I'd turn it off. Less than one minute!!! I made myself get into the habit of turning the phone off after receiving the mail. A common habit is reading the new mail while the phone is still on. This ends up costing money and losing air time. When the last new mail would come in, I would completely disconnect and put the phone away in its box. Then we'd all take turns reading our mail.

We all got into a rhythm of life at sea. The days began to blend together. Whoever had the 4:00 – 6:00 AM watch was greeted to a sunrise. Usually two of us were awake during the day. Often all three of us enjoyed being out in the cockpit together. We now could relax and enjoy the sailing.

The steering was easier once we were out of the Gulf Stream. The winds had come around to the southwest, blowing on our stern quarter, putting us on a broad reach most of the rest of the way. This point of sail is most sailors' favorite. It happens when the wind is basically on the side and back. If the wind moves towards the bow, it's called a close reach. Wind right on the side is reaching. Broad reaching is easiest and most pleasant. It's better than dead downwind. Plus it's fast and fun. At times we had winds over 30, but mostly around 15 – 20 knots. Perfect. Sometimes waves the size of houses simply marched on by. They were accompanied by sunny skies or starry nights and didn't appear threatening. Since the waves were far apart, their height was not an issue.

Generally, sailing is pretty simple on *Tenacity*. The jib was our most used sail. It is a roller reefing jib and is very efficient thanks to Robert's sailmaking talent. We had an inner forestay installed before we left to hold a storm jib, but we discovered the reefed jib actually was a more efficient sail in heavy air. We had made a decision to take the main sail down before dark and sail through the night with just the jib and mizzen. We decided to do this to avoid a possible situation where we would have to rush out at night, in the dark, to take down the main, which is a physical job even for two people. Our boat does have bright deck lights, but we felt better to be safe than risk a possible injury. If we had to reduce sail quickly in the middle of the night, it was immensely easier to reef the jib than to deal with the main. The jib and mizzen alone proved to be plenty of sail. Sometimes, when the wind would flirt with the 25 - 30 knot range, we would reef these, and we still made good speed.

Robert insisted if the steering got to be too difficult while he was sleeping, that we should knock on the cabin top and he'd come out to help reef in the jib, much easier with another pair of hands, and could be done in the safety of the cockpit. One day, John and I were outside, John was steering, and we were talking and talking, comparing notes on a variety of world topics. Robert was catching up on sleep. While John and I were yakking away, I noticed Robert's hand emerging from one of the aft cabin's hatches, and the hand trimmed in the mizzen. Even asleep Robert was tuned in!

Night watches were time for solitude. Night watches were my favorite, but the hardest to finish. For three hours, it was just me and the ocean out there, under a dazzling display of sparkly diamond stars in the dark sky. Steering would keep me busy the whole watch. But those last 30 minutes were so hard! We all had tricks to keep our eyes open for the final stretch. I had finished the trail mix and coffee beans during the first two hours and couldn't get more. I would rise up and down on my toes and count, or check on the chart plotter right in front of the wheel. We turned it off at night because the screen was too bright. So every now and then, we'd turn it on and check our status. At the end of the three hour shift, the relief person came out. Robert was after me, and seeing him emerge from the companionway was a joyous moment! In fact, the joy started when I'd see the light come on in our cabin! When he came out, I'd unhook my safety harness, give him the update on the conditions, go below, take off all my gear, and crawl into the bunk. Crawling into the bunk after a windy night watch was truly a reward. I'd be asleep before my head hit the pillow.

Between watches, there was reading, e-mailing, checking on boat things, cleaning, sleeping, exercising, lots of conversation, solving the world's problems, and eating. With the exception of dinner, food was make what you want. We were on our own for breakfast, lunch, snacks and the addicting midnight trail mix. But I did make a hot meal for dinner. It was the one time of day when we were all together. It was our happy hour! A social event!

I tried to make something interesting every night. I wanted to make meals that could be eaten with one fork, since putting a plate down to use a knife could end up in a disaster should the boat lurch. Also, table space was at a minimum as we chose to eat outside in the cockpit.

I would think about what I was going to make for dinner during my earlier watches, after checking inventory and seeing which fresh foods were holding out. I'd start with chopping garlic and onion. I used all three burners, (in spite of advice in sailing cookbooks telling readers to use only one burner). We dined on meals ranging from pasta carbonara, Moroccan chicken tagine over rice, to beans and rice with sausage, and shrimp scampi. I made an attempt to get green food in every meal, with fresh veggies, frozen veggies and eventually canned. Some meals were more memorable than others, but all were good.

On day 15, I wanted to make Italian meatballs, pasta and tomato sauce. I had taken the ground beef out of the freezer that morning. We still had plenty of onions, herbs and garlic, and I would need to use canned tomatoes, but still, I planned to make the sauce from scratch. I got the water going for the pasta, and chopped the garlic and onion and heated up the oil. I put the beef in a mixing bowl along with breadcrumbs, basil, oregano, salt, pepper and an egg and mixed it up. I made perfect sized meatballs and put them in the pan once the onions were soft and the oil sizzling hot. They started to brown and when I went to turn them, they completely fell apart into a mass of hamburger helper! Oh NO!! This was a disaster! I had ground beef mush all over the pan and not one intact meatball! I was so upset! I didn't even notice Robert and John going on about how good it smelled. I held back tears and continued to add the tomatoes and pasta as if it was a normal meatball dish. Sulking, I handed out the beers, utensils, napkins, Parmesan cheese and then the bowls of mush. I was still pouting when Robert handed me his empty bowl and asked for more! "That was awesome," they both said! And to top that off, that evening we saw a green flash! So we named my mush meal "Green Flash Ground Beef."

Sometimes I made cookies and cake for dessert. Once in while I would make a hot breakfast if the weather allowed. One of my favorite breakfasts was beer bread, a perfect bread on a boat. It is so easy. Just mix a can of beer with flour, some sugar, a little baking powder, and bake it for about 45 minutes. The beer provides the yeast! No kneading and no rising. Just mix and bake. The beer flavor cooks out. It tastes like fresh bread. Sweet if you want to add more sugar. It is a most wonderful experience to eat hot beer bread with butter and jam along with fresh coffee while the sun rises over the ocean.

Tenacity was a good "fooder."

We had a "rule" of one beer a day. And it was a wonderful beer! In the beginning of the crossing, I would reach into the fridge and among a variety of beer, I'd see a Natty Boh can left over from Tim's wake, and I would ask if any one wanted it. "In honor of Tim," Robert would say, "I'll have the Natty Boh." One day I saw the last Natty Boh. "Last one," I announced. But the next day, I spotted another one. I said, "OK, THIS is the last Natty Boh." I was sure they were all gone, but then one evening, you guessed it, I saw another one! Was Tim up to this? This went on the entire two years. We didn't drink Natty Boh every night. In fact, we don't even like Natty Boh. I cleaned the fridge several times and swore there was no more Natty Boh. Then I'd see one in the fridge! How did I miss it? I would use it to make beer bread if no one wanted to drink it. Then again I'd open the fridge and see another can of Natty Boh with that cartoon on the can of the little mustached guy winking at me. We thought this business of the "One More Natty Boh" was finally over. But then in April of 2013, when we were already home, Casey was in town and stopped by to hear about our adventure. I offered him a beer, looked into the fridge, and wouldn't you know it, I saw a can of Natty Boh!!! I believe THAT was the final one. This is why the story of Tim's service was significant, and I promise, I SWEAR, I am NOT making this up!

We did have a couple of hurricanes to contend with. Tropical storms, actually, but with names. We skirted them both, but we got a little bit of rain and increasing winds. Nothing that we couldn't deal with. One was named Cindy and one named Bret.

Blog: When Cindy Met Bret

July 23 2011

38:72.00N 53:10.50W

Bret is a determined storm, very methodical, doesn't take chances, and spends more time glued to his computer watching FailBlog Videos on YouTube and less time enjoying the great outdoors. Cindy on the other hand likes to run! She wanted to see the Ocean and all the beautiful skies that come with it! So she asks Bret to go North with her. But he doesn't listen. And he plods along at his pace, completely unaware of the spectacular moons, the megawatt stars and galaxies in the night skies, the wickedly cool clouds with weird copper colors, brilliant rainbows, oozing sunsets, sunrises that look like medieval dragons, even the dolphins leaping and playing in his path. That Bret, eyes glued down, no sense of adventure, doesn't even respond to Cindy's invitation! So Cindy said "See ya" and zoomed up rapidly towards the North laughing out loud leaving lots of sunshine in her wake. And Bret basically fizzled out. Leaving not even enough rain to fill one lousy laundry bucket!!!! It looks like Bret is not a Threat. Sounds like a song sung by the Temptations.

And so you have it, the Tale of Two Storms.

CHAPTER 12

Feline Fun

Our two cats were born from a feral mother on my studio floor in April of 2008, and moved onto the boat with us as soon as they were weaned. They view the boat as their home and their sanctuary. They've been sailing for two years around the Chesapeake Bay and seem to be OK with sailing, but hate motoring.

Sailing was different in the ocean. Besides the fact that there was much more motion than a normal day on the Bay, we didn't stop at night.

Perkins, the girl, was the first to emerge from hiding. She took solace in lying next to me during the July 4th storm with the 60 knot winds, or maybe I took solace in HER lying next to me. Either way, she was out of a hiding hole and on the bunk. We watched in amazement as the next several days revealed her discovering her" sea legs." At first it was one small step, and stop, and sway side to side, while she looked up at us as if to say "Is this right?" Then it was two steps, then many steps. Then she was jumping up onto another surface. At first she had a hard time gauging her jumps and nearly hit the cabin's overhead during big bouncing waves, but she got it and got very good. She soon wandered around the boat as "normal," as normal as a cat who walks sideways can be. It was a very cool sight.

But all this time Dabola was still in hiding. He wouldn't come out. He needed to eat and drink. We tried coaxing him out with Temptations, which finally did work but after many days already at sea. And when he did come out, Perkins was there looking at him. I know animals communicate, they HAVE to. If I could have filled in the "words" spoken on that day Dabola came out, it would have been:

Perkins: "Come on out big brother, don't be so scared."

Dabola: "I'll just wait till they stop. I'll be fine."

Perkins: "That's the problem. They don't seem to be stopping any time soon."

Dabola: "You're kidding, right?"

Perkins:"Nope."

Dabola: (sigh) "OK, how do you do that weird walk?"

Dabola emerged. One foot at a time. He took little steps, and looked up at us with his big questioning eyes, until he could walk all the whole length of the boat. Then he'd look up at us again, and walk back. Gradually he was able to move around with the same ease as his sister, sidestepping and rocking side to side. Perkins seemed to be much happier that she once again had her brother to play with. They were both running around, doing cat things, but with a "funny" walk. When they stood while the boat was heeling, their legs were at angles, and they rocked side to side as the boat rocked, only they rocked in the opposite direction of the boat. Like the gimbaled stove.

Now, when they weren't playing, eating, cleaning themselves, and other various cat activities, they both slept in our bunk. Purring contently. All the while plotting their revenge.

Blog: 1972 Buick Riviera

July 17 2011
38:10.41N 51:56.26W

I've been asked if my pets were celebrities who would they be? Easy! Perkins would be Audrey Hepburn, Dabola would be Dean Martin. And if I were asked if my pets owned a car, what would it be? Perkins would drive a 2012 Mercedes SL, yellow, and

Dabola would drive a 1972 Buick Riviera, rusted gold with crumpled Natty Bohs in the back seat.

If they had a boat, what kind of boat would they have? Perkins would have this boat! AS is!! She is loving it! However, Dabola would have a 1988 42' Silverton permanently tied to the dock. With cable TV, lawn chairs and a grill. All is well here. STILL beating into now East winds! I am ready for the "prevailing" SW winds already!!!!!

Apparently I make good food! Our most wonderful crew member John Prehn, who has crewed on many Merchant Marine ships, says this little ship is a good fooder!!! Made chicken cheddar pasta last night that was killer The fridge is back to 38 degrees. The warm waters in Bermuda kept it at 44. We have one, and only one beer a day. And it will be cold!

Blog: July 20 2011

38:10.41N 50:56.26W

It seems I made a mistake about my cat Dabola. If he had a boat, it'd be a 1967 57' Chris Craft Constellation, with hard top and obligatory blue stripe. More his style.

He came out of hiding yesterday and drank water, ate Temptations (what do they put into that stuff?) and rubbed his head against the bulkhead. Good signs. I really worry about him, but he seems to be doing OK.

CHAPTER 13

Musical Scores, Creative News and Starry Starry Nights

Sometimes I would pass the time during midnight watch playing tunes in my head. I had a complete midnight playlist. Often it would be old classic rock tunes that came to me in the moment like Don MacLean's "Starry Starry Night" or Eric Clapton's "After Midnight." Sometimes the tune in my head would be a fantasy of me playing a lengthy piano piece, like "Rhapsody in Blue." If Robert came out for his watch during my piano fantasy, I would say, "Hold on just a moment, I'm almost done with the last movement." Another way I passed the time was to compose my blog in my head. This evolved into my writing a fictional newspaper that I called "The Middle Of The Ocean Gazette," or "MOTO Gazette." Sometimes I would laugh out loud, to myself, alone outside in the cockpit in the middle of the night. I found out later my midnight chuckling could be heard and John and Robert would wonder what was I doing out there? One night, Robert was coming out for his watch, and I was laughing so hard I couldn't speak. I just unhooked my harness, shoulders shaking with laughter, and went below.

Middle Of The Ocean Gazette

37:55.00 N 57:03.00 W
July? 2011

Headline News

American Yacht Enters Azorean High

"*Tenacity,*" a 47' ketch hailing from United States' East coast, has entered the air mass known as the Azorean High, located near and around the Archipelago Islands, the Azores. This air mass is known for its very light breezes and sunny skies. *Tenacity* and her crew seem relatively unconcerned of their current location. "Makes for nice sunning," says John Prehn, The Most Wonderful Crew Member. Having had optimum sailing winds since leaving Bermuda earlier this month, this air mass brings slower progress towards the Azores, which is the next destination for *Tenacity*.

"We've had stiff breezes on the nose and then big winds behind us with huge following seas! As much fun as that was, it's a bit nice not to be thrown around so much down below. I may take this downtime and bake a cake!" says First Mate and Cook Cindy Fletcher Holden.

The Most Wonderful Captain Robert enjoyed employing an old sail called a "drifter" and was pleased to see it filling nicely in the light air. "We're up to 4 knots! and more." This also is a good time for the crew to go around the stable deck and inspect hardware. "We found major cracks in the triple sheave Harken mainsheet block, and we were able to replace it with the ease of working on a steady boat." says Captain Holden.

Not knowing how long they will be enjoying the Azorean High, *Tenacity's* crew will make the most of this time working on tans, catching up on reading, misc. chores and of course, eating.

Business News

Seas Not Safe for Serious Spenders

In days of yore, ocean going vessels were out of communication with their folks back on dry land. It's been said to many a cruiser, "you can't spend any money while you're at sea!" Well those days are gone with the advent of satellite e-mail! Now one can get a request via e-mail to "authorize" a sum of money on a credit card, simply by e-mailing back and typing OK. It's in fact easier than going to Amazon.com and accidentally hitting "add to cart" for another pair of platform stiletto shoes. So not even the wide open sea is safe for the addicted spender! For example, when the minutes on the sat phone threaten to run out, a warning appears from the provider. All you have to do is type "OK." More minutes are billed to your credit card just like that!

Police Beat

Investigation remains open in the mysterious case of the turning off of the refrigerator compressor. Considered persons of interest: Dabola and Perkins, cats who live aboard *Tenacity*. They are suspects in the potential loss of precious food, have been taken into custody and are being questioned. "These cats have clear motive, as they are counting their days in captivity, and cold food is of no interest to them," reports First Mate and Cook Cindy Fletcher Holden. What makes this case even more intriguing is the cats know exactly to the minute how long they have been held, and the crew barely knows what month it is, let alone day of the a week, or how many days they've been out here.

Obituaries

Sam Squid, of unknown address, died unexpectedly early one morning when attempting to, we're not sure what he was attempting, but he landed with a thud in the cockpit of *Tenacity*, and died on impact. Survivors are not known.

Frank Flying Fish, of unknown address, died of complications following a missed attempt to fly over a 47' ketch in the Middle Of The Ocean. He most likely survived the fall but died due to subsequent dehydration. His body was found the morning after. "He was doing what he loved," said his daughter, Freida.

One morning sunrise arrived along with light winds and we put up the drifter, a lightweight jib that can fill up in such delicate breezes. It was a beautiful morning and I made pancakes! We sipped coffee, ate pancakes and welcomed with pleasure another day in the ocean. We knew we would miss these days, and nights as well.

On nights when the moon was not so big, the stars were more

intense. The sky was filled with galaxies. John knew many of the names of the constellations and would point them out to us. We saw many shooting stars, some so bright they lit up the whole sky!

Blog: A Star To Steer By by John Prehn

July 26 2011
– 37:55:00 N 57:03:00 W

On passage-making boats, there are certain requisites; safety and comfort are primary.

And there are the desirables; good food and the refrigeration system to stock for that.

A self steering rig and that holy-of-holies: an ice maker.

The last two items we don't have.

Cold beer makes up for no ice, but the boat has to be hand steered every moment

it is underway. We knew this leaving Bermuda. With three aboard, we stand wheel watch,

three hours on, six off. And the steering demands attention; the relationship between

wind and wave, sails and rudder is constantly changing. To maintain our easterly course

the helmsman must balance all these forces. In some conditions, a moment's inattention

and you find that you're heading for Nova Scotia, or worse, you could put the rig in danger *from an inadvertent jibe.*

Surprisingly, the three hour tricks at the wheel
seem to go fast. In the sun or rain, in fair or foul
weather. Some nights can be a real wrestling match.
Some days, just a gentle tug on the
wheel will put things right. But always the demand
to be the helmsman, the balancer of
forces behind the wheel.

Except one night. That evening, the wind and the
waves, and the heading we were on,
with the set of the sails, no steering was needed. For
hours at a time the wheel went untouched.

I sat sideways in the cockpit, facing south. Instead of
peering into the compass for guidance,
I picked a star, Antares, in the constellation Scorpio,
to steer by. The night and sea rolled by.

I will most likely forget most of the struggles at the
wheel, the rain and the squalls.

But I will long remember that gentle night, when
the whole cosmos was in balance, and just
to the west of the glow of the Milky Way, I could
steer by a star.

Dabola and Perkins were beginning to actually like their new world. They would come out in the cockpit and watch the seas go by. We would not let them outside without supervision. These cats were precious! Once they stopped hating the motion, we saw them actually enjoy coming outside to experience the breeze, the sea sounds and sunshine. As long as one of us, and not the helmsman, could be there to watch them, we'd let them go out. We also tried to play with them to keep them fit.

The days kept going by. It seemed like one beautiful day blended in with the next. Many books got read and lots of food eaten. We had an easy time with our rationing system.

We were doing quite well on food and water. The diesel supply we checked every day. We used a long thin bamboo stick as our fuel gauge. It had every inch marked with a black line. This is more accurate than our electric fuel gauge, which doesn't work anyway. Later we would find out that every cruiser we met uses a manual stick. We even compared stick length, color and material. Even some of the newest finest yachts don't have working fuel gauges. I have no explanation for this.

Blog: Dangerous Items Onboard

July 26 2011
38:46.07N 41:08.46W

They say one of the most dangerous items on an Ocean going sailboat is a calendar!!! Or a crew with a plane ticket! I have lost sense of what day of the week it is, and have no idea of the date, off hand.

We are of course keeping an official ship's log, but my own personal method of keeping track is writing down what I've made for dinners. I can then count how many days we've been out and can bring up in my memory what was going on around us. Like while I made that shrimp scampi, we had one of the best sunsets, or clearing skies after a rainy day for beef stew, or sweet and sour pork after a splendid sunny day. Cooking is a gymnastic accomplishment. I've got it down!! We really need to video it! I don't believe in holding back just because it's a bit "rough". We are having some great meals and they are highlights of our days.

I am down to 2 onions. This is on the edge of tragic. I am now rationing onions. There is a quote in a book called "On The Wind's Way" by William Snaith, about an old classic Trans Atlantic sailboat race, where the author, who cooks, says "First you chop an onion, THEN you decide what to cook" and that's ME!!! So rationing onions is roughing it in my book. But we will survive!

We are getting close to Horta! I am already starting a grocery list!! (onions on top) At least we have plenty of garlic!!

According to the IMRAY Book of Atlantic Islands, there are "Hypermarkets" in Horta. Is this where we run around frantically looking for onions and act like we are totally out of time?

Oh yeah, I did buy shoes in Bermuda. Had to, it's my job.

Then, on Day 15, tragedy struck. We were down to one last onion.

I had to take a deep breath. I realized that now I really needed to ration this precious vegetable! And I did and we were fine. We still had plenty of spices and garlic, and sufficient food and ingredients to continue with "Café *Tenacity*, Offshore Gourmet Dining!" But, for a moment there, I was worried. Once I calmed down, I realized that in these days of calmer seas, I had more time to write in the MOTO Gazette.

Middle Of The Ocean Gazette

Weekend Edition
July ? 2011

Headline News

Science Agrees on Size of Seas

For decades, even centuries, scientists have argued over virtually every topic on Earth. Neither side being right or wrong, depending on how one looked at the subject. But it seems there will always be differences in opinion among the most educated and inspirational scientists. These differences spark debates and conversations that seemingly will never end. Like Nature vs. Nurture, Predestined Future vs. Free Will, God vs. No God, Global Warming vs. Climate Change vs. Government Conspiracy, and so on.

But after hundreds of years of Sea Faring, adventurers, ranging from explorers seeking new land, pirates seeking booty, merchant mariners seeking commerce and yachtsmen seeking speed, one thing that everyone agrees with, scientists and commoners alike, is that this Ocean is darn right big!

Business News

New Sea Product a Splashing Success

Ever Damp, a newly patented product offering the qualities of Life at Sea, is expected to hit stores from Europe to the United States later this Summer. A simple organic mixture of salt and water, Ever Damp can be applied safely to clothing, linens, hair, skin and even food, to mimic the constantly damp sensation that comes with sailing for days in a small boat in a big Ocean. One doesn't have to spend hundreds of thousands of dollars anymore to experience one of the richest qualities of life at Sea. Product developer, Cindy Fletcher Holden, says "It's a factor of life out here that you just don't get on land. Even with hatches open and sun shining, every thing has a certain dampness to it, that I felt should be shared with the folks who don't get to sail offshore."

Ever Damp will come in a variety of sizes, and there may be a new line of Ever Damp Aromas, such as "Late Summer Mildew," and "Milk Turned Bad" and more.

Sports News

New Fitness Center Opens in the North Atlantic

Just opened sometime last week is the North Atlantic Athletic Club, aboard "Yacht *Tenacity*" offering a wide variety of training routines suitable for every competitive sport imaginable. NAAC has a complete resistance band workout that can be done while on watch in the cockpit, a portable elliptical in the main salon, hand steering which is a whole body workout when the winds are up, jib grinding, main sail raising, extreme cooking and as always, weird yoga.

To date, no official competitions are announced, but a Feline Race to the Aft Cabin is in the works. It appears that the moment the engine starts, the 2 Ship's Cats race to the aft locker defying all gravity and normal cat speed. The NAAC will announce when this race is official, and when betting can begin.

Community News

Baking Cakes Takes Top Priority in Azorean High

Crew aboard the American Yacht *Tenacity* are still enjoying plentiful sunshine while motoring through the high pressure air mass known as the Azorean High. To pass the time between tanning and watch keeping, first mate Cindy Fletcher Holden has already baked three cakes, two loaves of cornbread and is contemplating cookies except the boat seems to be out of vanilla extract. "Could be worse," says Fletcher-Holden, "At least the fridge is running! I can figure out how to go without vanilla, I'm sure." There was a short scare when the fridge was discovered turned off at the compressor, but all is back to normal now. Still a mystery. The main suspects as to the cause of the compressor being turned off, are the cats, who have been plotting their revenge now for weeks. "I wouldn't put it past them" says The Most Wonderful Crew John Prehn. "They're probably back there keeping score of days in captivity."

But all in all, motoring in a straight line while auto pilot, nicknamed "Bubbah" steers is a nice little break from 12 ft seas and exhausting hand steering.

"We even saw a green flash at sunset the other day" says Fletcher-Holden. "Very cool. And we saw two whales yesterday! Also very cool!"

Entertainment News

Celebrity Sightings in High Seas

Tom Hanks, Matt Damon, Cameron Diaz, Julia Roberts, Angelina and Brad, Bruce Willis, Harrison Ford, Jack Nicholson, Morgan Freeman, Paris Hilton, Leonardo DiCaprio, Johnny Depp, David Spade, Jack Black, Will Ferrell, Julia Stiles, Halle Barry, Sean Connery, Jane Seymour, Billy Bob Thornton, Cate Blanchett, Tina Fey, Kevin Spacey, and Matt Lauer were not present today in the Middle Of The Ocean.

During the last few days the winds got lighter. We kept the main sail up a few nights, and we still were going pretty slow, so we decided to motor. We were in the Typical Azorean High Pressure. To this day, many fellow sailors ask us if we sailed all the way or motored the last couple of days to the Azores. We did indeed motor. John had grandkids who were about to arrive back home in Annapolis from Germany, and he wanted to see them. Sailing in such light air could take many days and we had plenty of fuel, as shown on our bamboo stick. So we turned on the engine and plowed ahead.

The excitement to arrive in the Azores built by the hour! Conversation at dinner was quite chatty. We were making bets on exactly what day we would arrive, and bets on what time. We started to crank up music, knowing the engine was charging the batteries. Lots of smiling. We were getting close!!!

By Day 17, our GPS was reading estimated arrival time at less than 24 hours! We were sailing again in a bit more wind, enough to turn off the engine. During the night, the wind lightened again. I had the 3:00 – 6:00 AM watch along with my obligatory and addictive trail mix. At 5:45 a.m. I saw the lights of Faial! I tapped the cabin and woke up Robert. We would turn on the engine soon, but not yet. It was 5:45 Bermuda time. We didn't know what time it was here, but it was still dark, too dark to arrive, and besides, we wanted to relish this moment! I made coffee. We slowly sailed along at a whopping two knots. John got up. By dawn, we saw the island rise up out of the horizon! The sunrise was yellow and sweet! The top of the island of Pico, just a few miles from Faial, was peeking out from clouds. As the sun grew higher and the sky turned bluer, the island of Faial became closer, clearer, and quite green, dotted with white buildings and orange tiled roofs. Dolphins came over and escorted us around the bend and towards the harbor of Horta! By 9:00 a.m. Horta time, we were tied up at the immigration seawall. August 2, 2011. *Tenacity* made European Landfall!!

We had crossed the Atlantic! Well, we still had almost 1000 miles to mainland Europe, but we crossed a major part of the ocean! We had tenaciously endured many pitfalls, boat problems, weather issues, people issues, cat attitudes, paranormal beer and rotting potatoes. Now we were safe, healthy, happy, and on our boat, which was whole, sound and in the Azores! Even though we had reached this milestone, we knew that this adventure was just beginning.

CHAPTER 14

Hello Horta!

"You know what they say about this place," said Duncan Spencer, owner of a marine hardware and service center called Mid Atlantic Yacht Service, the only chandlery in Horta. I did not know what they said about this place. We had just gotten there, and were looking for a new mainsheet block and a 220 volt battery charger. "Europe doesn't get any better than right here," Duncan continued.

This is what they say about Horta. This was on Day One. Our adventure had a long way to go before we could agree or disagree with Duncan.

After checking in with immigration and getting our official Portuguese passport stamp, we were safely tied up in a slip. It is amazing how quickly life gets "normal" after spending 18 days at sea. It was a matter of seconds, not hours or days, but seconds after the dock lines were tied and the engine turned off, that "stuff" materialized all over the boat. In the ocean, every single thing is secured. The boat could have rolled over and nothing would be out of place. But now that we were at a dock, books, magazines, maps, and paper receipts found homes an any horizontal surface. Shoes showed up on the floor instead of in lockers. Jackets were flung on bunks and chairs. Chairs were no longer tied and stowed. Pens, sunglasses, coffee cups, backpacks, tools and cat toys were everywhere, not neatly stowed away like when we were at sea. Later, talking to other cruisers, we learned that this is common to all of them, no matter what the native language is!

Once settled a bit, I went for a much anticipated run, and Robert and John went in search of the marine hardware store. Then we went in search of wall space.

The town of Horta has become famous for its painted seawall. Sailors paint the names of their boats along the harbor's concrete wall. Over the past few decades, the harbor has grown substantially and so has the amount of seawall space to paint. In fact, the painted names, THOUSANDS of them, are not just limited to the concrete wall, but are every where, on the walkway under your feet, on benches, on wall tops, in wall crevices. There is hardly a blank spot of concrete. So finding a place for *Tenacity* was a challenge.

Robert, John and I finally decided on a spot that revealed a very old and worn name. No guilt painting over it. Our spot was next to stairs going up to the main road, a few yards away from the marina café. A good location. John and I wire brushed the surface and applied a coat of primer. Once the primer was dry, we laid out the design. I should again note that John and I both started our careers painting names on boats. So here we were, two professional sign painters ready to embark on this name painting tradition.

We discovered in our search for space a huge number of professional looking names painted here. How many sign painters sail across the ocean? Without knowing the answer, we continued with our mission. I hand drew the name "*Tenacity*" and we both applied a coat of quick dry sizing, a clear glue for gold leaf to stick to. Yes, I wanted to have *Tenacity* in 24 ct gold leaf, and after looking at thousands of other jobs, we did not see one other gold leaf name. (John and I both know the difference between gold leaf and gold paint). People gathered to watch.

Once the sizing got tacky, we applied the squares of gold to the letters. The audience grew. We could hear many comments in countless different languages.

Horta is a major stop for ocean crossing sailors and they come from all over the world. June through July is prime time for sailors to be there. The marina was full. We had arrived right at the beginning of the town's annual maritime festival called "Sea Week." The marina was busy, nearby streets were crowded with locals and tourists and international sailors. We had many onlookers by the time we were in the "gilding" phase of the project.

Once the gold was laid, I took over the rest of the task and painted dark blue water around the letters, (a sort of backwards way of painting but we wanted the gold to be applied to the white primer). Then I painted sky above. In the next few hours, I completed a whole vertical painting of *Tenacity*, the boat, sailing in the North Atlantic in perfect weather conditions, with the 24 ct gold lettering below. Under the gold leaf lettering I painted the names "Robert, Cindy and John, Dabola and Perkins," followed by "Annapolis, August 2011." We soon learned that word had gotten around the marina of our art work and that our wall painting of "*Tenacity*" was unofficially voted the best!

Days later we learned from other sailors that yacht owners often pre-purchase professionally cut stencils for the Horta wall. This helps explain the "professional" quality we saw in so many names.

During the final stages of the painting, I was visited by a young girl, Marie, who had also just arrived by boat with her family from South Africa. (An upwind sail in prevailing northerly winds). Marie was so enchanted she could not stop staring at me while I was painting. I offered her an art lesson. We met and quickly bonded with her parents and planned to have Marie over the next day. Marie arrived clutching her favorite kit of drawing supplies, a book on fairies and a huge smile. This was the first of what would become known as "Art Days," art lessons with children that we'd meet in marinas. While teaching Marie about drawing and color, I started some small pieces of art on paper, scenes of Horta and our surroundings. I was painting again.

John had to leave us the third day. We were of course sad to see him go, but were grateful that he stayed with us so long in spite of all the adversities. I was happy he could at least stay for the wall painting. He was wonderful crew. Soon it was just Robert and me, and Dabola and Perkins.

Our cats were so well behaved we felt they must have understood us when we would ask, or tell them, to please not get off the boat. Our fears were many. Getting lost or hit by a car to name a few. We know cats are amazing at finding their way around, but we have also heard horror stories of cats "visiting" another boat that then takes off! We buttoned a screen in place over the companionway to keep them in. When we forgot to close the screen, they stayed on the boat. They actually seemed proud to "guard" the boat.

We toured the town of Horta by foot. We talked about cruising to another island, but decided to stay a little while in Horta. We were falling in love with this place!! One day we splurged and hired an English speaking taxi driver, Antonio, for a tour of the island of Faial. Virtually no public transportation or tour buses exist on this island. We learned that a taxi tour was cheaper than a rental car.

Antonio drove us all over the island. We stopped often to get out and walk around. We saw the amazing walls of blue hydrangea that Robert had mistook for stone walls 30 years earlier only to discover that they were flowers as he got closer. Faial is known as the "Blue Island" because of these aromatic petal packed beauties. The flower walls wrap around rolling hills of lush green grass. Some of the flower walls act like fences for the many cows. The Azores is famous for its cows and their butter and cheese. Even in mainland Portugal and Spain the best dairy products are from the Azores.

We toured the area some refer to as the "Newest Land on Earth," due to a massive volcanic eruption in the 1950's. Much of the lava formed a large spit of new land, and much of this same lava covered existing land, covering whole villages in a dusty brown dirt, instead of the shiny black lava found on other volcanic islands. No one was hurt back then, but thousands of people left the island to new homes in the US or Europe because of this eruption. We dug the ground with our feet and spotted some orange tile from a roof of somebody's home. Spooky.

We were lucky to have sunshine as we reached the caldera (the top of the volcano) after driving up very steep and winding roads. Antonio said usually there are clouds sitting up there often completely blocking the view. I guess we brought good luck!

Back at the marina, we would pick a direction and go walking all over, relishing every moment on this delicious island. Some of the roads were so steep, walking up was a challenge. I wondered if the cars had special parking brakes or transmissions. Walking down was actually harder. But we loved every minute. We walked all over town, checking out every shop. We quickly discovered these shops close between 1:00 and 3:00, every day, and are all closed on Sunday. Welcome to Europe! We walked to the back side of the harbor and discovered the beach there and all the cool hiking trails beyond it. We hiked through every neighborhood in every direction, soaking up the full flavor of this town. And of course, we visited the grocery stores, becoming friendly with the small portside store's cashier, as well as discovering food finds at the huge supermarket (called the hypermarket) a mile away.

Not being wealthy, and on a budget allowing for two years of no income, we immediately realized we would have to do without certain foods. Chocolate was over $8 for a tiny bag. Peanut butter over $10 a jar and Parmesan cheese was over $12 for a tiny pouch. Those items, among a few other things, would go on our list of what not to buy. But no worries, we now had Nutella, the European chocolate spread, cheap! And we had Azorean cheese, which I now think is some of the best cheese in the world. It was everywhere and not expensive. And, the wine! We never paid over $2 for a bottle of wine, and GOOD wine, for the next two years.

We wanted to learn Portuguese. And grocery shopping was quickly becoming a good lesson in our new language. Our Portuguese would get better as time went on, but also harder. The dialects were proving vastly different from region to region, even on one island. But we were determined. During the course of our adventure, grocery stores would become some of the best language classrooms. One time I came out of a store grinning from ear to ear. Robert said, "What's with the big grin?" and I said, "I just had a complete conversation in Portuguese, with not a word of English!"

I fell in love with the old European buildings, with their iron porch railings, fancy window details and layers of peeling paint. We loved the cobblestone streets and cobblestone sidewalks with artistically inlaid black and white cobblestones, all made from lava. We walked up and down, north, south, east and west, sometimes just to the store, sometimes miles and miles. This would be the beginning of what would become our daily "walkabouts," another favorite part of the adventure. The old streets would become a lasting subject in future paintings.

The Sea Week festival celebrated all things maritime and traditional. There were regattas, boat parades, street vendors, Azorean traditional dancing, and lots of food and music. The feature bands played at night, some until the wee hours of the morning. One night we went up to the bandstand to be a part of the crowd, and we danced in the street to the flavorful local sounds. Being amateur ice dancers, we look like we know what we are doing when we dance, and people clapped for us. It was a good night!

One day, we heard some incredible orchestral music coming from the street. We went up to investigate. It was the Lisbon Symphony Orchestra rehearsing on a small stage. Incredible! Such big music right there! We waltzed right up to the stage and asked when they would be actually performing, and were told it would be the next night. We also learned that the Lisbon Symphony would team up with the local Horta Town Hall Big Band, to close the whole Sea Week on the final night.

We had quite an engaging conversation with the conductor. The conductor of a European Capital City's orchestra! He was very friendly. We wanted to share our excitement with someone. We invited our British neighbor, Rhonda, to join us for the next evening's concert. She did and we were treated to some fine music.

Several days later, on the final night of Sea Week, after the last performance, the conductor, who we met and felt we knew, invited us for a drink at one of the Sea Week's temporary "cafes." A conversation about instruments and who plays what arose. Robert explained that he plays flugelhorn. After a few more drinks, the conductor invited Robert to come to the next performance in another town to play his horn. Whether Robert felt shy about his horn skills being up to a major international symphonies' level, or the fact that the town in which they were headed was over 12 miles away and we had no way to get there, is up for discussion. We did not join them. But the invitation was special enough! Robert was invited to join the orchestra without any audition. Amazing what a few extra cocktails can do.

We had met our neighbor Rhonda in the slip next to our boat a few days before. She had sailed to Horta with her husband Mike from southern Portugal. They were British and they had relocated in the Portuguese city of Lagos and operated a canvas/sail loft there. Mike and Rhonda sail every summer to the Azores, but this summer, their loft got so busy with work, Mike had to fly back to Lagos to work while Rhonda stayed on their boat. Rhonda and Mike have completed one circumnavigation, as well as countless long passages, and they introduced us to our now favorite weather web site called "passage weather." They had the experience to know this was the most reliable weather forecast they had found. We felt such relief learning about this new great tool, and not having to rely on a weather router for future passage making. This web site is great. You pick the area you want to see, and it shows you a variety of color coded information, such as wind velocity or wave height. Light or no wind is white. Light to 10 knots is a light blue. 10 – 15 knots is a slightly darker blue. 15 – 20 is dark blue. 20 – 25 is bluish green, and then it gets greener, to yellow, to orange, to red and up to magenta. When the color for wind velocity is magenta, the wind is hurricane strength. You can see the colors from across the room! So I could be looking at the screen from 10 feet away and see yellow and maybe orange, and would say "we're not going there!"

We would pair up again with Rhonda and Mike on mainland Portugal. Our friendship became strong.

CHAPTER 15

Cows, Birds and Art Shows

One day Robert and I took a ferry to the closest island of Pico, and spent many hours walking alongside vineyards and miles of short lava stone walls, the shiny black kind of lava, that surround acres of grapes for Pico's own wine. We walked along tall feathery grasses, dusty red roads, charming cabins, and the black sandy lava coastline. Pico is a beautiful island, but we didn't think the harbor was protected enough to go by boat. As we were pulling back into Horta on the ferry, we spotted Laurie and Neil, the couple we met in Bermuda. They had made it to Horta! Across the ocean in their 28 ft Triton! We were truly excited for them. We asked about their crossing and at one point asked if they had seen a green flash. They said they never saw the horizon. Their boat was too small to see over the waves! Wow!

Laurie and I bonded right away. She is a talented photographer, and knowing that I am a professional artist, she invited me to their boat to critique her photos. I had to pinch myself to see if this was real. Here we were across the ocean on a European island, on our own boat, and I was engaging in fun art lessons with kids and intellectual photo critiques with an adult. Laurie and I also took long walks looking for subjects to either paint or photograph. I did start a few small paintings and made a joke that we should host an art show, and have a reception, complete with wine, cheese and music. Ha Ha Ha. But Laurie did not take this to be a joke, and said, "Yes!! Let's do it!!" Me and my big mouth.

In order to pull off an art show, we had several hurdles to clear. One was for us each to complete a body of work for a show. I would have to do several more small paintings, which at this stage were a combination of pencil, ink and paint on paper. Laurie needed to select and print the photos she wanted to exhibit. Then we needed to find a location. We spent a few days in search of a good spot and finally decided to "borrow" one outside wall of a huge white tent that was temporarily set up for the Sea Week Festival, right there in our marina. With Robert's help, we came up with a plan that consisted of rigging leech line around the corners of the tent, and using clothes pins to hang our photos and paper paintings. It would be a consistent looking exhibit. Then, we decided on a date, August 27, several weeks away.

During all this artistic planning, Robert and I were in touch with a potential crew member, Philip, who we found on the internet before we left Annapolis. We reconnected once we arrived in Horta and Philip made arrangements to fly out to join us for the sail to mainland Portugal. His plane was set to arrive on Faial on the 26th just in time for the art show.

In spite of how much we were loving Horta, we still wanted to see another Azorean island. We had a few free days before Philip and the art show. We sailed to the island Sao George. Only 22 miles away, Sao George is also volcanic, but instead of being formed by one enormous eruption thousands of years ago, it was formed by many small eruptions, and as a result, the island is long and narrow, high in the middle with the sides steeply sloping down to the sea below. We stayed at a small marina in the village of Velas, snugly situated beneath tall dramatic cliffs. In these cliffs live a breed of bird called Cory Shearwater. These birds, for whatever reason, are found on Sao George, but not Faial, even though the islands are close to together. We think that the cliffs attract the birds. At dusk, which was around 9 p.m. in late August, the birds launch into a frenzy of mating calls. A sound like nothing else, except maybe obnoxious computer games, which I thought it was, coming from a neighbor's boat. But then I realized it was these birds! After a few minutes, I absolutely loved the sound! I couldn't get enough and was sad that it only lasted about 30 minutes. We later learned some of the locals have the birds' sounds on their phone ringtones. I want this ringtone!

As I mentioned before, there are a lot of cows in the Azores. You can walk to a grocery store, and as you walk out, there might be a cow standing right there! We're told there are more cows than people on some islands.

The cows are free roaming and are not afraid if you approach them, which is easy since they are everywhere. The islanders get so much milk from these cows they can't bottle it fast enough so most of the milk is in boxes. In fact, it's hard to find cold fresh milk! But even the box milk tastes outstanding. Is it the grass that makes this stuff so good? The cheese is mouth watering "eyes roll back in your head" good! We visited a cheese factory on Sao George and almost had to be dragged away from the free sample table. We bought a lot of cheese.

We saw a lot of cows on Faial, but even more on Sao George. And we would see even more on Terciera! Good thing we love cheese!!

Blog: East River Tugboat Captain

Aug 16 2011
38:32.00N 27:45.19W

I grew up on power boats. One of my first memories was sleeping on the engine box of our 22' Chris Craft. My Dad had that boat when I was born. We always had some boat.

I had some "lessons" on the 42' Chris Craft that we had during my elementary and junior high school years. That was a tough boat to maneuver because it always seemed to have one engine down. I learned how to "side walk" it using one engine and forward and reverse gears. But I didn't get good at this until later when my Dad bought a 1966 19' wooden

Century speedboat, with a 350 HP inboard engine, and separate handles for throttle and gear shift. I got so good at handling this boat, people thought it had bow thrusters. I truly could get into a "zone" and put that little 19' boat in a 19' 2" space without having to throw a line ashore. Dad said it looked like the little boat was an extension of my right arm. I loved handling that boat. If I had a parallel life, I think I'd want to be a tugboat captain on New York's East River.

It's been a while since I've been in that zone. Robert is the professional sailor, but he lets me do all the docking. And I've been put to the test a few times in these European marinas. And let's not forget Bermuda and the big concrete seawall. We had to move the boat in Horta from the entry seawall to a tight slip, and then out of that tight slip into another less tight slip, but a tight entry to the slip. It gets really tight here. Very crowded. Lots of boats rafted up. Our South African friends had a really tough time getting out of the marina. There were 6 people helping, although I'll bet they could have gotten out easier if no one "helped," if you know what I mean.

Then we went to Sao Georges and tied up to the sea wall after marina hours, and in the morning, they put us into a nice wide slip, but right behind the slip were boulders. Big rocks. Big hard solid pointy rocks. Right there. Within spitting distance from the aft deck.

I knew we were safe in the slip, but while touring the island, I worried about backing out of the slip. The boat backs OK, but it can be tricky in windy conditions. The worst scenario was for the wind to be blowing into the little harbor and blowing us into the rocks while backing out. And OF COURSE, right as we were getting ready to go, the wind picked up blowing right into the harbor! Thing is, we had to leave to get back to Horta to get ready for new crew, so waiting was not an option! So I got into the "zone," backed the boat out with a hard port rudder, spinned the boat in its own length and merrily cruised out in forward gear.

Then we had to raft up once back in Horta. The slips were all taken. And again, I got into the zone and made a perfect landing, alongside one very cool boat named "Great Dane" from Canada.

We leave for Lisbon in a couple of days! I hope the zone lasts when we get there!

After a few memorable days on Sao George, we returned to Horta and got down to serious art show planning and promo. I finished up my little paintings on paper. I drew a flier to hand out. Laurie and I went to our local photo/print/copy shop and made prints of her photos, copies of my flier, and prints from photos of my large oil paintings, to add to the show. We then went all over town, handing out fliers and talking up the show. We bought wine (cheap), cheese (the best), crackers (of course) and proceeded to set up the show. Our new crew Phillip, who had just arrived, was enchanted with this whole thing. Neil, who happens to be an extremely skilled guitarist, offered to accompany our show with live jazz guitar. Laurie and I discussed our fashion strategy, limited after an ocean crossing, but we managed to dress up for the occasion. Then, there we were, hosting an art opening and PEOPLE SHOWED UP! It was a party! Complete with wine, live music and no permission to use the space.

Perfect! I even sold a painting.

One young woman was watching the party unfold from the street and came over to join us. Her name was Beta. She was a kitchen worker at the famous sailor's bar called Peter's Café Sport. Peter's started many, many years ago, as a gathering spot for ocean crossing sailors. Although now a popular tourist hangout, it is still an important place for sailors to know about to get assistance and information. For example, Peter's was the only place in all of Horta that would cash one of our American Express Traveler Checks. No one else would even look at them. Peter's Café is a much loved spot for cruisers. Beta, who loved our art show, insisted we all come over to Peter's Café for dinner, a bit of a worrisome proposition being that it was a Saturday night and Peter's would be packed. But we decided to go, and when we arrived, Beta had arranged for prime seating at a huge table for Robert, myself, Phillip, Laurie and Neil. It was a wonderful send off dinner!

CHAPTER 16

New Crew and The Last Of The Azores

Our plan was to sail to the island of Terciera, which is to the east of Faial, before heading across the rest of the Atlantic to Portugal. Neil had landed some paying work on a neighboring boat, so Laurie asked if she could join us for the trip. She would then take a ferry back. Absolutely!! So off we sailed, overnight, along with Phillip and Laurie to the port of Angra, in the city of Heroismo on the island of Terciera. We decided to stay at least a few days there to explore Terciera and watch the weather (at passageweather.com) for our next 900 miles of ocean sailing. This island looked like it had a lot to offer.

After a swim at the beach next to our marina, Laurie and I took to the streets of Heroismo in search of a ferry office to get her return ticket, as well as fun shopping. Ticket purchased, we continued to roam the streets. At one point we noticed a guy wearing an American style western hat, standing next to an ancient rusty white International Harvester pickup truck, trying to sell figs to a local lady at a fruit stand. This guy was speaking English with an American accent. An accent we had not heard since Virginia, with the exception of Laurie and Neil. He also heard us, and soon approached us asking where we were from. After some small talk, he informed us his name was Alan, and he was indeed American, and that he had bought a house there on Terciera and that his land had fig trees, LOTS of fig trees, and he couldn't eat them fast enough and was trying to unload them. So he invited us to come to his house and bring bags to fill with figs. Well, we had already planned to rent a car for the next day, so this could work. But instead of giving us an address, you know, like a street name with a number, he took our tourist map of the island that we got at the Ferry Office and put a black dot on a spot that supposedly marked where his house was. "It's about 10 miles outside of town," he said. "Look for a modern stone house with my truck in the driveway. It's on the coast." OK!

Easier said than done! He did give us his phone number, and Phillip had an international cell phone, but for whatever reason, Alan's number would not connect. We drove around and around in search of the black dot and finally stopped at a café to see if maybe their phone would work. It did, and we were so close to Alan's house we could walk from there. Alan greeted us and showed us in. Bags in hand, we picked figs while getting a full tour of Alan's incredible home and property, up on a hill over looking the ocean. He had seen us sail by! We kept talking, and in between sampling figs right off the trees, we found out that Alan had a plane ticket to Lisbon in a few days, but was not allowed to fly, doctor's orders, because he had fallen several days earlier, while picking figs, and hit his head and suffered a mild concussion. Although he was now fine, the doctors were reluctant to let him fly so soon. As the conversation continued and the fig bags filled, we also learned that Alan had sailing experience and next thing we knew, we were inviting him along to sail to Portugal!! Our intuition told us he'd be great crew, and later this intuition proved correct. He would become a life long friend and return as crew for future passages.

Alan loved Terciera and had really gotten to know the people and traditions. He told us about the bulls.

I already knew a little about the bulls. Back in Horta, in the photo store where Laurie and I made copies, I noticed a video playing up on a screen above the cashier. They were selling a video of the annual "Festival of The Bull." Not the running of the bulls like they do in Spain. And far, far from a bull fight in a ring. The local men attempt to "mount," or "ride" or "grab" or whatever "winning strategy" they might call it to "win over" a bull, a 2,000 + lb bull, that is being taunted by a 180 lb guy, holding a cheap umbrella and poking it at an increasingly angry horned animal the size of a Chevy

Suburban. The bulls, of course, get annoyed and charge after the guys, (as seen on this video, where the guys kind of make a quick stab at getting on the bull but then the bull practically plunders them.) I actually had to take my eyes away. Over the years, the town folks have put rubber tops on the horns to prevent impaling, and also put tethers on the bulls to keep them from running free and mad. But the bull ALWAYS wins! Sometimes the guys will run and retreat, often scrambling up some wall and hiding out on a window sill (one of the best postcards we saw was a bull standing on the street under a few guys huddling on a window sill, still clutching their umbrellas.) Other times the men are hurt. The hospitals remain ready and provide ambulances waiting at the roadsides.

Whatever started this rather curious event? Well, we learned from Alan that the roots go back to the 1500's, when the Spaniards came to conquer the island of Terciera. The local men were off fishing. So the women, afraid for their lives, let the bulls out of the pasture to run after the Spaniards, thereby saving the island. Alan's history lesson inspired the following blog entry which is my version of the true history of the Festival of the Bulls.

Blog: "A Truck Full Of Beer"

Sep 1 2011

Once upon a time, two guys from the Azorean Island of Terciera, Antonio and Sergio, scored a whole truckload of ice cold Sagres Mini bottles of beer. Now, there wasn't any refrigeration back then in the 1500's, so Antonio said, "Life's too short! Let's round up the guys and go fishing and drink this beer while it's cold!"

And so off they went.

Meanwhile, the women of Terciera were home busy making cheese, baking bread, milking cows and sewing aprons with the word "Acores" in different colors on the front.

And while the cheese was still draining, these Spaniards arrived by boat, full bent on invading and conquering the island. But the local men were not around to defend their land. So the women shared a collective eye roll and sighed, wiped their hands on their aprons, and proceeded to the pastures where the bulls were kept.

Now these bulls are important to the Azores. There are more cows than people, and they are important for cheese, milk, and butter. And the bulls are important to keep the cows populated.

And the bulls are huge and strong. And they don't particularly like shiny wiggly things. So when the Spaniards came charging up the hill, the bulls, now freed by the women, took one look at the Spaniards' shiny swords and wiggly fringe, and went full out after the Spaniards, heads down, horns pointing forward, hoofs flying, nostrils flaring.

The Spaniards did not expect this at all! And they fled! Running back to their ships where they frantically hoisted sail, yanked up their outboards and got out of there!

Then the women whistled for the bulls, led them back to the pasture, fed them, patted them on the back, and returned to the duty of cheese and bread.

By dark, Antonio, Sergio and all the guys returned home with their truck full of empty bottles of Sagres Minis only to find the women quite pissed. They were upset because the men weren't men enough to stand up to the Spanish, being as how they weren't even around during all the Spaniard/Bull stuff going on.

So the men needed to prove themselves to the women! Antonio had an idea! They would let one bull out of his pen, taunt him with shiny things or umbrellas, and take turns trying to "grab" the bull by its horns. Or even try to get on the bull's back. Which more often than not ended in the guys getting rather mauled. But this started a tradition that is still going on today. Guys still trying to prove their manhood by trying to take on angry bulls. This happens right out in the street. The bulls are loose and the guys get beat up, stepped on, bumped, butted and stabbed. It's an annual event called the Festival of the Bull. Over the years they've started putting rubber caps on the bulls' horns but the guys still get beat up. But they still do it! And at the end of the day, the women shoo off the guys, scratch the bulls behind their ears, pet their furry foreheads, put them back in the pasture, feed them, and go back to cheese, bread and sewing.

Now the men may or may not have proved their manhood after that one day when they missed the Spaniards, but the women are still doing their thing with the cheese and bread only now they also hire pool boys.

But they don't have any pools.

We continued our tour of the island, agreeing to meet Alan at the boat the next day, ready to go. On the opposite end of Terciera from our marina, is a port called Praia Vitoria. This is a major seaport that includes ships, ferries and a large popular marina. Laurie's ferry would depart from here. We parked the rental car and went walking to check out this other harbor. I noticed a familiar looking boat in the marina and realized it was Sea Jade, the South African boat owned by our Horta friends Martin and Henda, with their kids, Henna and my little art fan Marie! We decided to say hi, and as we approached their boat, Marie spotted me. She jumped down to the floating dock and ran full speed in my direction. I braced myself. I saw it coming. She ran full on at me and leaped up into a midair hug. Had I not been prepared, I could have ended up with a concussion from falling back. It was one of the most welcoming moments I have ever experienced!

After a great visit with them, we needed to get to the port so Laurie could head on back to Faial. Once Laurie was safely on her ferry, we "vittled up" and again were provisioned from the grocery store and a farmer's market. Alan came aboard, along with two watermelons, a couple of quart size bottles of Sagres beer, some perishable groceries from his house and a dozen bags of figs. it was time to head to sea. On Sep 1, 2011, at 7:30 p.m., we cast off the dock lines and once again pointed *Tenacity* east. It was time to finish the Atlantic.

CHAPTER 17

Some Wind, Some Sun and Some Swimming

It is amazing how much easier it was to leave the dock at Terciera, and head out to sea, compared to all the millions of hours of planning, working and fretting we did before we left Annapolis. Now it's just another hop across the ocean!

We were advised to stick as far north as possible, as the winds tend to go more north and build the closer to land you get. At first, as expected, we had light north winds, sunny days, great dinners. We were enjoying our new crew and the fact that we all got along so well. Alan discovered our movie collection and watched movies on his computer. One evening he brought his computer up on deck, and while we dined on chicken pesto and pasta, we watched the 1971 Steven Spielberg movie "Duel" starring Dennis Weaver, about a terrified guy (Weaver) driving a Plymouth Valiant, being murderously pursued for no reason by a tanker truck driver. It felt ironic to all of us to be watching a desert car crash video while surrounded by open ocean.

The wind lessened the next day and soon completely died, leaving us with glassy calm seas, reflecting the sky in perfection. Alan decided to go swimming. Robert and I also dove in. Philip decided not to. Swimming in the middle of the ocean was creepy!!!! Even though there was not a lick of breeze, the seas had a very gentle swell that you really couldn't feel on the boat. But while I was swimming in the water, down low, the rolling of the boat appeared amplified and seeing it being tossed from side to side was unnerving. Still, diving into the water that was thousands of feet deep was memorable!!

MOTO GAZETTE
Middle Of The Ocean Gazette

Sep.? 2011

Headline news

Tenacity Crew Jumps Ship

On day four of calms seas and motoring, the crew aboard the American sailing yacht "*Tenacity*" decided it was time to take a dip in the ocean. After carefully installing the ship's portable ladder (there was a horror movie about a crew who all jumped off a yacht with no way to get back on board) *Tenacity's* crew dove into the brilliant blue, glassy calm, salty and chilly water! "It's as warm as the air!" said crew Al, first in. "Bull S*%^t" said Cindy Fletcher Holden, second in.

Crew Philip decided to pass on account of he just had a nice shower. "I'll take photos," he said.

"I've never seen the boat at this perspective" said Fletcher Holden, "Not so much the angle but the boat's rocking is amazing from down here. It's funny how you don't feel it as much on board."

The portable ladder was a bit of a challenge but it did the job. It's no surprise that Captain Robert was able to climb up and down the portable ladder like a monkey.

After the delightful swim, the crew proceeded to crank up old classic rock and Eurasian Lounge tunes on the CD player while enjoying some of the end of the Summer sun.

But they hope some wind will fill in soon. "It's weird to see the Ocean this flat for so many days," said Philip.

Tenacity is headed for Lisbon and should be there in a couple of days.

Business news

Funky Footwear For The Savvy Shoe Buyer

Cindy Fletcher Holden, artist and self confessed shoe addict, has begun designs on a new line of painted leather clogs. Having done a few before, she says this time, the designs will be more monochromatic and less flamboyant. More able to go with anything, but still a little "out there."

The concept is partly inspired by a pair of inexpensive yoga pants she purchased before she embarked on a European cruise. The rest of the inspiration came from looking at fashions in store windows while in the Azores, Portuguese Islands about 900 miles West from mainland Europe. "The coolest thing is I can now spell Portuguese without spell check!!!"

Fletcher Holden will start her new line of shoes with her own Jeffery Campbell high heeled platform clogs. "This style clog is very in here in Europe, I had no idea! Hopefully my paint jobs will attract new customers."

She will post photos when they are done on Facebook.

Environmental news

Wallowing Whales a Welcome Sight for Weary Sailors

On Day four of motoring, the crew of *Tenacity* was delighted to spot two rather large and loud whales, right before a very beautiful sunset that included a rather small (blink and miss it) green flash. This was a very welcome sight! The whales did sort of a slow ride up and dive down, making big low grunting sounds. Very whale like. At first the crew thought they were dolphins, but soon saw how huge these creatures were and realized they were whales!!!!

The crew spotted a few turtles, (one baby), but also several sightings of some sort of plastic trash. "This is what makes us weary, not sailing," says Cindy Fletcher Holden, First Mate, cook, shoe designer and champion speller, "It's rather sad how much plastic sh*#t is out here. We've seen laundry baskets, parts of buckets, old buoy type things, stuff like that."

The crew of *Tenacity* keeps all its plastic trash in a separate bag to recycle once ashore. It's a job and a pain but well worth it when you consider how long plastic lasts in the Ocean Environment.

Once figs reach the fully ripened stage, they go downhill fast. We had pounds and pounds of figs on board! Once we got Alan and Philip adjusted to a two hour watch routine, the figs and what to do with them became a priority. I decided to make jam, and it was easy. I just cooked them with water and sugar until they became a thick spreadable goo in the pan, and I transferred this to jars and we had delicious fig jam for almost the whole sail from Terciera to mainland Portugal.

We motored a bit after the swimming, dined on great meals, and fig jam. We discussed world problems, solving a few, read books, watched more movies, read and sent e-mail, napped, played with the cats, sunned, and soaked in the final 900 miles of sea. After our bizarre swimming experience, the winds filled in nicely!

Blog: Almost There!

Sep 7 2011

38:16.18N 11:40.53W

Now we are in a healthy NE wind with plenty of sunshine but chilly air! Just to think 24 hours ago we were swimming!

According to the GPS, we should be arriving at the shipping separation lanes tomorrow morning, about 8:00 our time. Which is good because it will be daylight. And then it's another 30 miles to our first Portugal stop, a town called Cascais. Which has a good sheltered marina and is a short train ride to downtown Lisbon. It's actually a suburb of Lisbon.

So tonight will be my final West to East Ocean Dinner. (Pasta and Azorean sausage) and after that my last middle of the night watch, which I've grown to really like. Again with the stars, and moon, alone outside surrounded by sea, I will never get tired of that! I will miss that! But will be experiencing it again on the way back!!

Once in Lisbon, we'll be checking out the sights, and talking to locals about other sailing destinations along the coast. I will be scoping out some outdoor murals there and have begun the process of talking about mural jobs. I already have two possibilities. But I won't jinx it by talking about it more!!!! Also, may look into renting a "garagem" (Portuguese for garage) to possibly rent to do some painting. Or we continue sailing towards Madeira and Canaries and home. We'll see!! What I'd REALLY love is to revisit the Azores in the Spring, and then head to Madeira, etc. I feel like I'm not done with that place. Like I've left unfinished business.

But that is for later to decide. Right now, I need to relish being out here, curl up with my latest book, make dinner, stand watch, wobble around the cabin, enjoy the salty air on my face, the sea critters, the amazing sunset, the big waves, each with character enough to name them (there goes Leroy!) the sound of the water whooshing by under the power of the sails, instead of the engine. ALTHOUGH we LOVE OUR

ENGINE!!!!!! That thing goes and goes and goes...I expect to open the engine room door and see a big pink bunny banging a base drum in there!!! (kudos to Jeff at Bay Shore Marine for a terrific rebuild)!!!

Today we cranked up lots of music. I turned Alan onto Eva Cassidy! He turned us onto some very cool music from Turkey, a CD called "360 Lounging" from Istanbul. For those of you who know me, just the title alone is my style of world lounge music!!

So, next stop, "The Continent." Maybe dinner out. I'll dress up! I have the shoes!

We sailed through busy shipping lanes as we approached commercial activity. Philip says to this day that this was his favorite part! I slept through it. Funny, before we ever left, one fear I had was sleeping through something big like "landfall." And here I slept through a situation that was a highlight for someone else. But I can't bring that day back.

On September 8, we spotted land. And I was awake! Europe! We had made it the whole way across the Atlantic. Continent to continent. And the funny thing was, we were still "home" since we brought our "house" with us. We sailed closer to shore and then navigated into the river Tejo towards the harbor of Cascais (pronounced "cashKEYE"). We were once again safely docked after a long passage at sea. No one hurt, the boat whole, the cats purring.

We had achieved a huge goal, crossing the ocean on our own boat. All the preparations, expenses, planning had worked. We not only had a safe crossing but an enjoyable one. What we did not know was where life was going to take us next. Waiting for us were more adventures that didn't even involve sailing! Adventures that were about culture, history, new friends, music, food, skating, cats, dogs and even a donkey. Our trans-Atlantic sail was the means to land us in a new world of surprises and what are now cherished memories.

Blog: Cascais Landing

Sep 9, 2011
38:40.00N 09:25.00W

We are docked safely in a marina in mainland Europe. Portugal to be exact. City of Cascais to be more exact. At the Marina De Cascais to get a bit anal.

Cascais is at the mouth of the Rio Tejo. Lisbon is up the river a bit.

The wind filled in quite nicely and we were able to sail on a close reach the last 30 hours of sailing, in a healthy 20 –25 knot NE wind. We crossed the busy shipping channel this morning right after "sunrise" (it was windy and cloudy, no sun) and then the sky gradually cleared and we had a beautiful sunny breezy entrance into our first European River!!!!!!!!!

Two perfect landings, one at the reception dock, and one in our slip. I was in the zone.

Our boat looks right at home at this first class marina!

So the next step is to go up river and find a bit less first class, ergo, less expensive marina! But for now, we are here relishing in the fact that we crossed the entire Atlantic Ocean! 3000 plus miles under our now salty belts. Time for a long shower and champagne!!

CHAPTER 18

Continental Europe

Cascais is an absolutely charming old seaport on the mouth of the river Tejo. The marina is big and modern. We arrived just after the America's Cup tryouts. There was an attempt by locals to arouse interest in yacht racing. The marina houses many shops and offices selling high tech racing gear. The whole experience walking around the marina grounds felt like visiting the Annapolis Sailboat show. Interest in yacht racing there is growing. Cascais has a way to go to become an international yacht racing hub, but it's coming.

A short walk away from the marina took us into Cascais's Old Town. The sidewalks have a wave pattern in the cobblestones that can make you dizzy, or maybe it was all that sailing. Many tourists flock to Cascais, and the wavy cobblestones are one of the many attractions. We decided to celebrate our successful voyage and eat out. We chose an outdoor restaurant called "Dukes" right in the heart of town. It was next to a public square, that became a stage later in the evening when a guitar player joined up with a singer and entertained us all with high energy Portuguese and Latin music, all live and acoustic, and really good. It didn't take much prodding from Alan and Phillip to get Robert and I dancing to the music. We even got applause! What a great way to spend our first day in continental Europe!

After a couple of days there, we ventured up the river, joined by Isabelle, a friend of Alan's. We tied up at a marina in a part of Lisbon called Alacantura, and I found it hard to believe that we were on our boat, in a European Capital City!!! Lisbon is huge and famous, and there we were. Right downtown! Alan and Phillip hung around a bit, touring and exploring, and then it was time for them to head on back to their own lives. They were good crew.

CHAPTER 19

Just the Two of Us

Now it was just Robert and me. In downtown Lisbon.

Long before we left, we were advised by other sailors who had done similar trips in Europe to find a place to winter over. One guy even used the words "hunker down." We poured over cruising guide books, internet articles and other books to pick our place to hang for the winter. Most of these places were down in southern Portugal. We still had time to get there. It was only mid September and we had Lisbon to see. But this marina was not cheap. We spent just a couple of more days there, taking advantage of the subway and trains to see the city, and then decided to explore up the river to a known, safe, and free anchorage in the town of Seixal, just up and across the river from Lisbon.

This anchorage is described as "quiet" and "convenient" in the cruising guide, and it lives up to its description. But they could have warned us about the tide!! We anchored in 19 feet of water, according to our depth sounder, and it was a bit disconcerting to have the boat pointing into the current, instead of pointing into the wind, but we held good and strong. It was time to extract the dinghy from the lazarette and go exploring! We dinghied around the anchorage and met a few other cruisers, including a fellow we had already met at the Cascais marina, Tony, another American who had sailed all by himself from New York. Amazing, these guys who solo. Tony had hit a partially submerged mooring buoy and messed up his prop, and would be hauling out at a large yacht yard near our anchorage. We had read about this yacht yard in the cruising guide and made a mental note to go visit the next day.

After the dinghy ride, a sunset dinner, and a good night's sleep, we awoke to see men walking around our boat, wearing high rubber boots, carrying a variety of buckets and clamming tools. We were now in nine feet of water, still afloat, but just a few yards away, it was mud!!! Good thing we didn't anchor in nine feet the night before. It was low tide when we spotted the clammers and we knew the water would soon come back. Still, we now knew we had over ten ft tides to reckon with.

We stayed at the anchorage a while. I even started a few little paintings on some canvases that I bought in Cascais. We met the guys who run the Tagus Yachting Center and were impressed with the extent of what their yard could do. We explored the little town of Seixal, got to know a few locals, and decided it was time to move along. We had heard about a marina in Lisbon suburb called Oerias, that was offering a half price stay if you crossed the ocean. So we checked it out.

The entrance to the marina has a tricky dog leg turn. It is common for marina employees to come out in an inflatable to help cruisers get into a slip, since it can be difficult due to strong winds and currents. The guys who come out are called "mariners" and our mariner was a guy named Henrique. I was driving the boat and was experiencing trouble shifting gears. Henrique got onto our boat and after quite a bit of struggle, we got into a safe slip. I was upset with my boat handling. Robert and Henrique said I did fine, that there was a 20 knot wind and very strong current to contend with, and that it wasn't me that made it so hard and not to take it personally. Still, it had felt wrong. I had become "one" with *Tenacity* when it came to maneuvering, and this time the helm didn't feel like the extension of my right arm as it had been since Virginia. I finally calmed down and let it go.

We felt at home with the folks at the Oerias Marina and stayed a few days. We studied our charts and chatted with the marina crew about their favorite places to stop on the way down the coast of Portugal. Before we left to head south, we checked all the fluids in the engine and discovered the gear box was dangerously low on oil and appeared to be leaking. So maybe it wasn't my imagination when I was having a hard time docking!! This was not good. We decided to call our new buddies at Tagus Yacht Center to see if they could check out our gear box. They said to come on over. We left Oerias and headed back to our anchorage in Seixal. Rafael at Tagus said to anchor for the night, and then come in early afternoon with the rising tide.

This would give me time for a morning run along the waterfront of Seixal before we went to the yard. I had already established a route and was accustomed to the friendly nods from the locals who hung around the town beach. But when I went to get into the dinghy that next morning, I saw the dinghy line had been cut. Our dinghy was gone! Gone! Stolen! The line was clearly cut. This was bad.

Robert called Rafael with a new cell phone that we picked up in Cascasis for local calls. We thought we could see what looked like a deflated dinghy on the little beach, and asked if Rafael could help us by taking us out in his skiff to see. As we approached the beach, the town locals, the ones with the friendly nods, were waving their arms yelling "Aci! Aci!" (Here! Here!) and sure enough, it was our dinghy. We learned through Rafael's translation that the locals saw the thief bringing our dinghy in to load into his truck. They said the thief wasn't from their town. And they recognized our dinghy, knew it was stolen and shooed the thief away! So we got it back, minus the gas tank, but we got it back! This was good.

After many thanks, hugs and handshakes, we continued with our day and headed over to Tagus.

CHAPTER 20

Life in a Boatyard

Rafael, and his cousin Sergio, the owners of Tagus, are part of a family run shipyard business that started generations ago at the end of the river where we were anchored. They are young and eager to work and help. The yard's mechanic was out of town. They offered to let us stay there, and have an outside contractor from Lisbon came in and look at the job. (They made an exception for us to allow an outside contractor – we were becoming friends). We were concerned about whether or not the gearbox needed to come out, and if we needed to haul the boat to do this. If we had to haul the boat, we were in the right place. We would wait until morning when the Lisbon mechanics came to make that decision.

During the crossing, we allowed the shaft to spin. We had inquired about this way before we left and were told different theories about letting it freewheel, or installing a brake. The answers were split down the middle. We chose the free spinning. One advantage was that we could hear the speed increase from inside the cabin. But it was possible that this is what caused the damage to the oil pump inside the gearbox. It was also possible that it was simply age. Our solution from this point on would be to tie off the shaft with an expendable string, we used a shoelace, and if we had to start the engine in an emergency, it would just break off. This system would prove just fine in the future. But for now, we needed to get the pump fixed.

Rafael noticed my new paintings and a conversation started about portraits. I mentioned I could paint his two year old daughter and his eyes lit up. He worked out a sort of barter, we would still have to pay whatever the Lisbon guys charged, but Rafael would let us stay at his yard for the duration of the work, and only charge us his cost for any parts. Also, he would let me use a spare room behind the office as a studio to paint his portrait, and whatever else I wanted to paint. It was actually not a bad deal. From this point on, he bent over backwards to help us. Amazing what a portrait will do. I went to work and practically moved in to the spare room.

The mechanics arrived the next morning and successfully removed the gear box without having to haul the boat. That was the good news. The bad news was a bearing was shot and the gearbox may need to be rebuilt. So they took the transmission to their Lisbon shop.

There we were, at Tagus Yacht Center, for an unknown amount of time, unable to move! Some may have seen this as an unfortunate place to be stuck. The neighborhood, a small town called Amora, was not what you may call "pretty." It was a working class suburb of Lisbon, a bit untidy. It had several nondescript apartment buildings with their fair share of hung laundry, some city streets with basic stores, and an abandoned park still owned by a group of tired activists trying to keep the struggling Portuguese Communist Party alive. Along the waterfront, when the tide went out, the aroma was, well, let's just say "interesting." But in spite of all of this, we grew to love this place!

We quickly found the grocery stores and were set with that logistic. We soon bonded with Tony, the solo American sailor we had met before. He was waiting for a new prop. An evening beer with Tony became a daily routine. We grew to really enjoy his company. I was making excellent progress on the portrait (Rafael's daughter has red hair and blue eyes! like me! Very rare in Portugal) and I started several small canvases. We did chores around the boat. Robert decided to buy and install a European inverter that would allow us to plug into local dock power, charge our house batteries, and use our 110 volt appliances. This was now especially relevant since our engine was inoperable for the time being.

By day four I had established two different running routes and started to see some of the same folks every morning out on their bikes, or running as well. We went on evening walk-abouts. We met the local animals. We were becoming locals.

One local animal was a donkey that was a mascot at a school for girls that we passed on the way to the grocery store. This donkey was well taken care of and as soft as a bunny with huge brown eyes and long lashes! He looked like a Disney character! We would stop and pet him, and I would buy him a carrot for our walk back from the store. One day, while we were petting our new friend, a local man walked by and pointed to the donkey and said "Jimantsu," the Portuguese word for donkey. This guy could tell we "weren't from around there." I said "Jimonzoo?" He shook his head, "JiMAHNTzoo." I said, "JiMAHNTzoo?" He smiled and nodded. Pronunciation is tricky in Portuguese. Robert and I returned to the boat, walking and practicing our new word, saying it over and over ".Jimantsu, jimantsu, jimantsu......" We must have looked a bit odd. Imagine seeing someone walk down your street saying "donkey, donkey donkey."

The gearbox needed a part that was coming from Spain. Ok, fine. But when Tony heard this, he smiled and said he was still waiting for his prop, also coming from Spain, and he was on week two. We might be here a while! I kept working on the portrait and all the little paintings in the "studio." Robert did chores on the boat. We shopped, did laundry, all the usual, and we hung with Tony for a "happy hour" in the evening. Then we met Theo.

Theo had sailed his miniature ship from Holland four years earlier and ended up at Tagus in need of some work. (four years????) but he stayed on purpose (whew!) Theo sings Fado music. Theo stayed in Tagus because of Fado music. Here's the thing. Fado music is so very Portuguese. It is as Portuguese as country music is American. It is similar in words, but very different in melody. Like country music, every Fado song sounds kind of alike. The tunes are haunting and sad, melodic and beautiful. Heartfelt singing is accompanied by a guitar, and the words are always about a longing for something gone. The Portuguese word for this longing is "Saldash," and it's hard to translate. One theory about the origin of Fado says it was started by the women whose men left to go to sea to fish, and didn't return. In current Fado, the words, like in our current country music, tend to be about getting jilted, or breaking up, or maybe Mama in jail and the pickup truck dying. Whatever the detail, it's manly sad, but not always.

There are many "Fado houses" in Portugal, especially in the Lisbon area. A Fado house is a restaurant, or a cafe that features Fado singers. In Lisbon, some of these Fado houses are famous tourist attractions. In towns like Amora, there are Fado houses for the locals, not tourists, and you can sign up and take a turn singing. Theo can sing, but he can't speak Portuguese. He speaks English with a solid Dutch accent. He somehow memorizes the words to Fado songs. They must sound odd to the Portuguese but he sings them anyway. Four years ago, when he first arrived in Amora, he put his name down at a local Fado house and got up and sang. They loved him, and he soon got some serious "gigs" in downtown Lisbon! Reporters covered the story and a Lisbon television ran a special about him. There he is, living on his boat, still hauled out at Tagus, riding his bike to the ferry, heading into Lisbon for a night of Fado singing!

We discovered a local Fado house near the boatyard and went with Theo and Tony one night. For 15 euros, you get an appetizer, soup, a whole entree, dessert, coffee, all the wine you can drink and the Fado entertainment!! All the wine you can drink? They automatically bring out large carafes of wine and put them on the tables and refill them, like water! Funny – if you want water, you have to ask the waiter. Wow.

Theo put in his name. They already knew him there and he got warm greetings when we arrived. We ate, drank, (wine) and listened to an evening of great Fado. When Theo got up to sing, the audience laughed and clapped hard. We think his versions of Fado were not the sad ones! He was a big hit, as always. We applauded the best we could after several liters of free wine.

Life at the boatyard became more and more fun. We got to know the whole gang that ran the yard. We learned that the Tagus Boatyard was previously called the Venamar Shipyard and that the two businesses now both operate on the same property. The shipyard was originally started by Rafael's and Sergio's great grandfather. Their fathers are still there working, even though they could be retired. They come every day, hard hats on, and keep busy. One of them, Sidonou, really bonded with us. When he saw the finished portrait of his granddaughter, he teared up and hugged me! He also would smile when we attempted to speak Portuguese. In the morning they say "Bom Dia" pronounced "Bon DEEEa." It's almost sung. Then after lunch (not afternoon) they say "Boa Tarde," pronounced "Bo Taahhhrd." Very little "R." Often they leave off the "Boa" and just say "Tahhhhrd." In the beginning we would say "Bo Tard," and Sidonou smiled that kind of smile that made us know we got it wrong. He gently corrected us, and we did get it right, saying "Boa Tarde" finally with a proper Portuguese accent. This proved useful later!!!! Also, we learned from him that it had to do with the mid-day meal, not the time on the clock. So, if he said to me "Bom Dia" at 4:00, I'd know he had worked through lunch. Which, in Portugal, is very rare. Lunch, often lasting three hours, we would soon learn, is a sacred time of day, but not for the shipyard guys. Their work is often dictated by the weather or the tides and tides don't stop for lunch. Those guys work their butts off.

The actual grounds of the shipyard were full of boat parts, ship parts, wooden crates, saw horses, scaffolding, tires, old engine parts, anchor chain, metal tubing, rigging cable, chairs, an old washing machine, jack stands, cinder blocks, old canvas, tarps, lots of sand, flower pots, a few dogs and Jimmy the cat. We could get internet access in the Venamar office up by the road, where there was a comfortable room with a couch and some tables. The walk from our boat to that office took us through all this boatyard eye candy and it was a real treat to see so much stuff, but still, in spite of what looked like chaotic junk, (beautiful in my eyes) the guys there ran a tight ship and got things done.

A couple arrived at Tagus to have their boat hauled for the winter, and they tied up next to us for the wait. He was Ola, from Sweden, and she was Torren, from Norway. They loved our happy hour with Tony and easily joined in our daily ritual, bringing beer, and sometimes a little bag of olives, or cheese to share. We arranged some chairs around the Tagus office and even found an old table. All we needed was an umbrella and we'd have Café Tagus. One evening Theo brought his electric keyboard, a nice one, full length (88 keys), with all the state of the art sound effects. I provided the musical entertainment when the keyboard was available. (Theo saved his singing for Fado houses.) One night we had a barbeque complete with the keyboard and Torren's guitar. It was live music featured that evening at Café Tagus.

Blog: Amora

Oct 2011
38:38.09N 05:06.00W

We have made new friends with the other boat people here. One, Tony, an American, left today. He's sailing to Madeira. We will miss him. Another, Theo, the Dutch Fado singer, left for Holland (by plane) today. We miss will him too. A couple from Sweden, Ola and his Norwegian wife Torren, are here on their boat. Last night we had a barbeque in the boatyard complete with Torren playing her guitar and me playing a very impressive electric keyboard that Theo let me borrow all week. Wow! What a machine! No cheap little toy. This keyboard is almost as long as a piano and has an amazing range of sounds. And it is really loud! After several days I felt like Keith

Emerson!! Or Rick Wakeman!! I will really, really miss this instrument.

We've totally gotten to know the whole gang that runs the yard. The guys that work in the yard had been watching me complete the little paintings for the Art Between the Creeks show, when I was using the spare office to work, which is where they go for 3:00 break time. (There is a coffee machine in the room. Little tiny cups of intensely strong coffee is what they all drink at break time). They also saw me work on a design for a mural I might be doing in Italy. It is so cool to try to talk to them about art and working as an artist. I will miss them very much.

My new running friend, Rosalea, is actually on her bike. She is riding slowly nursing a back injury, so I am able to run along side. She is a Philosophy professor, and has perfect English. She is from Sesimbra, where we might stop on the way to the Algarve. She now lives here in Amora. We just met last week and we've already had lengthy involved conversations about everything from politics to history, health, culture, you name it. I've learned a lot about life in Portugal through our conversations. And again, she has been a help with my struggling effort to lean this language! I will miss her.

We've reached the time of year when we have to really pay attention to the weather. Our new favorite web site is passageweather.com. There is a very impressive weather event marching down from Ireland this weekend. After Amora, we may have to hide out *somewhere, perhaps back in Oeiras, and wait out this big thing. 40 –60 knot winds out of the SOUTH. Absolutely the wrong direction. Tony was excited to get out and start heading south before it reaches here. All the boat people talk about these weather related things. We have become a bunch of "weather heads."*

Back when we were in Oerias, we had taken a bus to a city called Sintra, high up on the coast just north of Cascais. We loved Sintra so much we decided to go back since we were still stuck there at Tagus. We rented a car and spent a whole day visiting this charming village in the tree filled mountains, with several colorful castles that look like Disneyland, but real. It's an intoxicating place! Steep cobblestone streets with ancient archways led to flower covered old stone walls, complicated decorative rod iron railings, and orange tiled roofs.

As we drove into Sintra, we spotted a large building that had a banner out front reading "Hockey Club de Sintra." Hockey? Ice hockey? Could this be an ice rink? Holy cow! We found an ice rink? We pulled in to the parking lot and checked it out. It was closed. No one was around. But boy, it sure had ice rink written all over it. I even spotted what looked like the door for the Zamboni to come out. Sintra is a wealthy part of Portugal so an ice rink would not be out of the question. We peered in the front door trying to find some sign of ice. There were posters of hockey, showing guys on the ice with skates on. It was looking hopeful! Our hearts were racing! We saw a lobby and could sort of see a rink but didn't have good view from the front door. So we pulled out our laptop, which for whatever reason we had along with us, and our portable "dongle" that we bought to get emergency internet. And this was an emergency. We Googled "Hockey Club de Sintra" and it's roller skating! With inline skates! On a concrete floor. Oh well. Almost. We loved our long day in Sintra nevertheless.

One day Robert was moving our dinghy's new gas tank and hurt his back. Bad. He had back issues long before and they were mostly solved, through surgery as well as physical therapy, but now he was hurting and it wasn't good. The boatyard gang was worried for him. Sergio empathized because he had spent a year bedridden due to his own back problems and took Robert to his doctor for a cortisone shot. It helped, but didn't solve the problem. Robert was able to continue to do things, but now he was in pain, and walking became difficult.

We found a doctor through a recommendation from my running friend Rosalea, who would ride her bike slowly with my while I ran. She told me about her doctor in Lisbon and how her back condition was improving quickly. We called him and made an appointment. We would need to take the ferry into Lisbon, so we made a day of it. The hydroplaning ferry was an adventure itself. (I was thinking that I would love to get a job driving one. I am still thinking this). The doctor (his name is Dr. Robert) worked on Robert and we both felt he was in good hands. We made another appointment.

Finally Tony's prop arrived, one month and one week since he had hit that mooring ball. Also, our gearbox was finished. The morning Tony was ready to leave, we took our boat out see him off, but also to check on our new gearbox. Tony was safely on his way but our newly rebuilt gearbox was leaking oil. So we headed back with the news. The mechanics were able to stop the leak, and finally, after our month long stay at Tagus we were ready to go.

Before we left Annapolis, we had a farewell party, and my sister Jackie presented us with a large poster that said "have a good voyage" in three languages: French "Bon Voyage", Portuguese "Boa Viagem" and Pittsburgese "Git Atta Tan" on both sides. We used one side for our Maryland friends to sign farewell messages, and then we saved the other side for our new friends that we would meet. We had this poster neatly rolled up and safe inside the boat. I had forgotten about it until we were getting ready to head out of Tagus. I found it and yelled "Robert!!! The poster!!!" So we gathered all the gang on the dock and asked them to sign our poster. To our delight, they thoroughly enjoyed this! Rafael stood holding the pen to his chin clearly thinking what to write. Each guy lined up for their turn. It was precious. Rafeal's uncle Sidonuo wrote and wrote and gave us such tight bear hugs my eyes almost bugged out.

Then we finally cranked up the engine and motored away, and looking back, we saw the whole gang waving and snapping their cameras and cell phones. I swear we saw tears in Sidonuo's eyes.

CHAPTER 21

Where to Spend the Winter?

We returned to Oerias. They still had that half price deal going on. We knew we liked the marina and the staff, and it was close to Lisbon for the doctor appointment. When we pulled into our slip, a perfect landing this time with no outside help, thanks to a new gearbox, we arranged for an early morning taxi to take Robert to the train to head into downtown Lisbon for his second visit with Dr Robert. I went along for the adventure. We were getting to love Lisbon. It is a big bustling European city with much diversity. Some of the city is ancient and medieval. Some parts date back to the 1300's. Some areas are so modern they look like the Jetsons cartoon. We decided to stay a bit to see this doctor at least two more times. Robert was already making progress!

We left Lisbon by train toward Oerias. As we were returning to the marina, one of the office guys there, George, called us just to see how Robert's back was doing. We were touched he would be interested. We knew this was a good marina.

We were still pouring over charts trying to decide where to spend the winter. It was now late October and it was time to get serious. Our new friends who worked at the marina had lots of recommendations and opinions to offer.

The weather was getting cooler. The forecast called for cold air coming, down into the upper 30's. It was time to consider heat. Or head south. Our heater is a diesel forced air system that is nice because it keeps the cabin dry as well as warm. The actual heating unit is located under the aft bunk, next to the hydraulic steering stuff. When Robert went to hook up the heater, he noticed that the bronze arm, the one that snapped in half back in that tornado was twisted. Bronze is a soft metal and does wear out - remember that through hull fitting? This arm, although still working, was now a potential problem. It was a matter of time for it to either break again, or to keep twisting to the point of not steering. We decided to see if there was a welder near by. We asked our new buddies in the office and they recommended a welder in Cascais, a good friend of the marina staff named Paulo. We took the train and our twisted bronze arm to Paulo's shop and he said he could make a new one out of stainless, for about $1000, only it would take at least three weeks. (We've heard this same thing before). Well, there we were, in a safe friendly marina, that was charging us half price, and it was almost November. This was a fine place to spend the Winter. Friendly people, grocery store close by, quiet neighborhood, a beautiful beach right next to the marina and a 15 minute train ride to downtown Lisbon. We told Paulo to go with it.

Robert made a couple more appointments with Dr. Robert. We returned to Paulo's shop to check on the arm and to take some teak trim to his woodworker shop partner. We started talking with Paulo about all sorts of things, work, sailing, art, and at one point, I mentioned my painting and showed him my web site. His eyes lit up! He said he wanted a painting. A big one. He said he would trade his work for a painting. Deal. (This was becoming fun, using paintings as a currency). Paulo said he would buy the canvas. I told him to start thinking about what he wanted me to paint. We decided to let Oerias Marina know that we would be staying for the holidays. It turned out that we didn't have to pick our spot after all, it picked us.

Paulo showed up at the boat with a new large blank canvas. The canvas was so big we couldn't get it into the companionway. Oh no! I was prepared to work inside our boat but this was now a problem. I decided to ask the marina staff if I could "borrow" a space, maybe the little laundry room, to set up the canvas and work. Paulo went with me to ask. When we asked George about using the laundry room, showing him the canvas, he shook his head, smiling and said "I have better. Follow me." He took us to a spare classroom in the huge pool house that was closed for the winter. It was a wonderful room. It had heat, good lighting, internet hook up and a view of the ocean! My new studio! This was incredible!

Paulo decided he wanted a seascape painting of Cascais harbor with the Volvo Boat "Abu Dabi" featured in the foreground, since he had worked on it and it hailed from Portugal. I moved my painting stuff into the new studio and went to work, which included starting more small paintings. I had finished the other ones and had already shipped them back to Annapolis for a show. Many of them sold on opening night. Time to make more. Now I had a studio.

I should take a moment here to talk a bit about these paintings. We didn't know going into this adventure that not only would the paintings provide income, and act as barter, but they would also change the way I approach art. I mentioned my freelance art business, boat lettering, murals, etc. But my passion is oil on canvas. Big ones. Back in college, I started a series of drawings of engine parts and boat stuff, inspired by the original *Tenacity*. These drawings became paintings and over the years, they evolved into paintings of old trucks, old cars, and then vintage cars to now shiny cars. I became known in the Annapolis area as a painter of large canvases. The dramatic size makes an instant impact on the viewer. The cars are nearly life size and meticulously rendered. I never liked working small, except for commissions. A few months before we left I was offered a solo show at a well known Annapolis gallery, and although it was a great show, with a couple of paintings selling, I was sad that I would not be able to paint big while we were on this adventure. I joked about renting a "garagem" (Portuguese for garage) and painting a big canvas. But what happened instead was a surprise. I was liking painting small. Apparently so were my followers. I was inspired by our new surroundings - the old cobblestoned streets, funky crumbly walls with layers of peeling paint, scruffy cats hanging out on marble ledges, old guys having beers at a sidewalk café and things like this. I was getting hooked on these little paintings. This new studio was perfect for doing Paulo's commissioned piece and more little ones to sell later.

Meanwhile, Robert's back was getting better and better, and he could now walk without pain. The visits to the doctor were not cheap. Since he had made such progress so far, he didn't want to stop just yet. I decided to ask Dr. Robert if he want to barter treatments for a painting. I went with Robert to the next visit and proposed a portrait of the doctor's teenaged kids. "What a great Christmas gift for your wife," I said, and it worked!

We settled into a routine in Oerias. Unlike Amora, Oerias is spotless. There is a long public promenade along the beach that makes for excellent running. Lisbon and Cascais are close and easy to get to.

Robert got many chores done on the boat. He was keeping the boat not only in good order, he was making improvements and the boat was actually becoming nicer with each job he did.

We toured Lisbon, went on walk-abouts, and I painted in the studio. I connected the computer to the internet and played NPR news while I painted. Just like home. In the evenings, Robert would join me, bring some Happy Hour beers and get online. We even had a few feral cats visit while I painted. Just like home! We sailed 3500 miles, to be "Just like home." However, it was Portugal, on the other side of the ocean.

Our friendships with the marina staff grew. They helped us with Portuguese. I got better at asking for things at the grocery store. I tried to ask for a whole turkey for Thanksgiving and realized they didn't know what Thanksgiving was! Oops. The Portuguese do cook whole turkeys at Christmas, but at other times, it's very hard to find one. We bought duck (frozen) instead, and it was delicious. We had a Thanksgiving "Skype" visit in the studio with family back home and then feasted on roasted duck, classic stuffing, mashed potatoes, green beans, the works! Our Thanksgiving in Portugal was quite nice.

Christmas decorations and shopping had already begun in mid November around Portugal. The place was getting festive! One night

Henrique invited us to his home for dinner. He said it was the first time he had ever invited a marina customer to dinner. We were honored. He served traditional Portuguese foods that were wonderful: balcahao (cod fish) salad and baked alhiera sausage. We told Henrique that we were interested in getting a live tree for Christmas but we noticed that there were no live trees available. It was December and we were getting ready for Christmas in Portugal. Henrique said he knew of a place where we could buy a live tree!

Blog: Christmas Tree Shopping

Dec 2011

38:40.06N 09:18.76W

Forests are not common in this part of Portugal. Pine trees are scarce. So the Portuguese decorate artificial trees for Christmas. There are plenty of these. In malls, they have artificial trees four stories high! In homes, offices and in stores, we have seen artificial trees that look real, and some that are shiny silver, pink, white, tall, skinny, short and fat. But all artificial. Nothing real.

So when our new friend Henrique told us about a place in the town of Perede that sells live cut trees, we were excited! Henrique offered to take us there in the marina's new shiny Nissan 4 door pick up, a perfect truck to haul our new tree!!

When my Dad was alive, it was a ritual. He and I would go to what ever Christmas tree lot he'd pick, and we'd do the classic thing of shaking the trees, standing back, checking them out and then picking the perfect tree for our house.

Robert and I have been continuing this tradition for over 20 years, either buying a tree for our first apartment or whatever studio I was working in.

The year 2001 was the first year we actually bought a tree for inside the boat. It was hardly a tree. Just a little thing. A "Charlie Brown" tree. But it was a real cut tree, that had a trunk and smelled like pine. It was small enough to put on a shelf in the boat, on top of built-in cabinetry. We strung lights on it and it was beautiful! Then the next year we spotted again a perfect little boat tree, along with the big and tall studio tree, and brought them home. Only the boat tree was too big for the shelf spot. So we made room in the corner of the cabin floor and put it up. Amazingly, there was still room to move about the cabin! And so it started, the live cut tree inside the boat. Each year it got a bit taller and a bit fuller, until we knew exactly how to pick out the perfect size.

We tried all different kinds of pines, loving each one. The collection of tree ornaments grew. Last year's tree was spectacular! Full of lights and ornament. Even the cats treated it with respect, barely knocking off more than 3 balls.

We've been doing a little shopping and we shipped off gifts for family. I've pulled out all the decorations for the boat and put a bunch of Christmas CD's in the CD player. But we still didn't know what to do about the tree. We really didn't want to spend money on a fake tree, not just because of tradition, but where would we store it? So when Henrique told us about the place in Perede that sells real trees, we were ecstatic and ready to buy our boat tree!

Perede is a sweet little town. A mix of old and new. Some winding streets, some hills, and close to the beach. I felt like a kid in the back seat of the Nissan, peering out the window looking for the trees for sale. I was looking for the string of lights around perhaps a section of a parking lot, or a giant inflatable Frosty the Snowman, next to a grassy lot full of trees.

But Henrique pulled up and parked next to what I swear is the tiniest RV trailer I've ever seen, with maybe 6 or so cut branches on the ground next to it. ?????????????????????????

These were branches!! I suppose if you squint, use your imagination, and maybe put down a couple of bottles of wine, they might begin to "resemble" a tree. But these were in fact branches. No trunks in sight.

We bought one anyway. We put our Christmas Branch in the back of the Nissan and headed back to the boat, with me sitting in the back seat longing for the string of lights around Frosty and the lot, and the mandatory tree shaking, trunk cutting and net wrapping tradition.

Our branch is sitting in a bucket of water in the cockpit, waiting for us to get its corner ready, where we will make every attempt to decorate it, and maybe it will look like a tree. Maybe. Wine will be needed. (plenty of THAT here)

So Merry Christmas to all! Happy New Year! And if you have a tree, hug it for me!!!!

Our passport was stamped in Horta on August 2nd, 2011. This meant we had been in Portugal for over three months. We should have gotten long term visas before we left, but we were so busy getting the boat ready it just never got done. So we had a regular tourist passport.

There is a relatively new law that allows visitors to the "Shengan" area to stay for only 90 days, and then after that, they need to leave for 90 days, and then can return. The "Shengan Border Agreement is between 26 European countries to allow Europeans to travel freely within this area. Outsiders have limits, for example Americans having 90 days at a time.

We were now in a difficult spot since we couldn't leave without our steering arm. We went and asked the immigration guy, Charles, at the Cascais marina. We met him when we made landfall there and he was super friendly. He gave us a two options. One was to make an appointment with the Immigrations Services office to get an extension. The other was to take a bus to Gibraltar, which is not part of the Shengan area, and get a Gibraltar Passport stamp.

We wanted to be honest and legal visitors so we made our appointment with the immigration office. It was a four hour wait in a crowded waiting room, and after making about a dozen new acquaintances discussing everything from books to food, we were at last seen by an official officer, a woman who was clearly having a rotten day. She could not see our Horta stamp in our passports because the ink was light (and she was partly blind). She proceeded to yell at us. "HOW DID YOU GET IN THIS COUNTRY?" she yelled as she jabbed at the passports. I felt my throat get thick and tears starting to well up. I squeaked "we sailed to the Azores by boat. They stamped the passports there." Then she put on her reading glasses (brilliant move). FINALLY she saw the stamp. Squinting through her glasses she "apologized" but couldn't give us an extension until we opened up a bank account in Portugal. Easier said than done.

We booked a bus for Gibraltar. We figured we'd have a road trip, see Gibraltar, get a stamp, and have a "mini vacation within a big vacation!" And besides, we knew there was an ice skating rink in Gibraltar.

We started the process of opening a bank account anyway, not just for an extension, but also a way to get cash and avoid costly international ATM fees. Opening a local account proved to be a long drawn out process. We decided to continue the bank business after Gibraltar.

The bus left from Lisbon in the evening and went through the night. We packed munchies and wine, and took along blankets and pillows. We arrived in the morning. We stayed in a sweet little hotel in a Spanish town called La Linha, about half the price of a hotel in Gibraltar. It was a short walk to Gibraltar from the hotel. After settling in our room, we headed to the "Big Rock." To enter, and exit Gibraltar, you walk across an active airport runway! Signs read "move quickly." So we did. But once inside the entry area, no one stamped our passport. We wandered around like lost kittens, passports in hand, looking for an official to give us a stamp. Finally we found a guy who gave us a stamp. He wouldn't at first. We had to tell him it was a souvenir! For what ever reason they had stopped stamping passports there. But we got our stamp. Then it was off to the rink.

We found the rink at the King's Bastion Center, complete with a restaurant, movie theater and shopping. The ice was rough because the Zamboni (ice resurfacing machine) was not working! So I slapped my hand on the counter, and said to the cashier, "we just sailed over 3000 miles to skate here!" He said we could skate for free. We did! We had the rough ice to ourselves for a short while and then a few skaters trickled in. A lesson was about to start and a coach saw us skating and hurried over to meet us. "We rarely ever see ice dancers here! Where are you from?" he said. We talked, and learned he was a former British Ice Dance Champion and was hired by the country of Gibraltar to be their main coach (how cool is that?)

We stayed a couple of days in Gibraltar thoroughly enjoying the visit, and when we finally left, there was no one on the Spanish side to stamp our passports. In fact, I swear the Spanish officer was napping with his hat pulled down and sunglasses on. Not that it mattered, it hadn't been 90 days, and we were already in "creative immigration status." It was basically a mess of a status. At this point our most recent stamp was Gibraltar and we were about to ride a bus back to Portugal. They don't stamp passports at bus stations. We would later learn that not only was our passport status a mess, but that the this law was not entirely understood and the law itself was also a mess.

Back in Oeiras, it was nearly Christmas Eve. The Portuguese celebrate Christmas Eve with a huge bacalhao/cod fish meal, music and gifts. And on Christmas, they have a turkey meal. I had been checking for days to make sure our local grocery store would have whole turkeys. (Voce tem Peru Entudo?) and they kept promising they would have more on Christmas Eve. On Christmas Eve morning, we walked to the store and got the very last turkey! The last one! If we had gone just a bit later, they would have been sold out. Unlike American grocery stores that have PILES of turkeys, both fresh and frozen, long before and after Christmas. We were lucky, and we had a great Christmas turkey dinner with all the extras including our decorated branch.

We searched the internet for ice rinks in Portugal long before we left Annapolis. We saw a few images of temporary rinks in Spain, the indoor rink in Gibraltar, a big indoor rink in Barcelona, but nothing in Portugal. When we asked around in person, we got shrugged shoulders and memories of little rinks in the past somewhere, Lisbon, maybe. It's just not a sport in Portugal.

One day we heard from a woman in Robert's doctor's office that there was a temporary rink in the town of Estoril, a short train ride from Oeiras, and it would be open until the first weekend in January. We decided to scope it out. Sure enough, we discovered an actual ice rink, about the size of a Range Rover, in a partially open tent. They were charging four euros to skate for 20 minutes. And there was a two hour wait! The tent was on a large open lawn just next to the train station. It was owned by a Brazilian company that put these rinks up for the holidays wherever they thought might attract skaters. Estoril is wealthy town with lots of diplomatic foreigners living there, so a little ice rink is a real treat for the Christmas season. But two hours to wait? We noticed several adults, some dressed silly, helping little kids stand up and skate, and pushing some of the kids around on bright orange plastic seals. I found the manager, Pedro, who spoke perfect English, and told him that Robert and I were trained instructors of ice skating back in the USA and our students were mostly little kids, and would he need any help with the kids in trade of ice time. Me and my big mouth! Next thing I knew we were on the ice pushing little kids around on plastic seals! Just like home! We revisited the rink the next day arriving early enough to get good fresh ice (they only cleaned it once in the morning.) We had a chance to sort of skate. The rink was so tiny that after two strokes, we were at the other end. Still, it was skating! We even had some success with teaching a few kids the basics. We tried to speak Portuguese, but the kids told us to stick with English.

The days that followed consisted of getting the boat ready for moving again. Paulo finished the steering arm and I finished his painting. Robert was pain free and could walk miles now! I finished Dr Robert's painting. We were doing quite a bit of boat maintenance. The marina informed me that they would need my "studio" soon. They were going to turn it into two offices and had to do some carpentry work inside. I needed to clear out. A bit sad, but it was a good thing while it lasted. It was time to move on.

We finally were successful in getting a local bank account. It took more red tape than we could possibly imagine, but it was done. A hardworking young guy named Jao bent over backwards to help us. He made sure we had everything in order, an ATM card, e-mail communication, even mail sent back to Annapolis. We still communicate with Jao to this day as a friend! Now we were able to use local ATM machines for cash, and would have this account when the time came to get a passport extension.

We had gotten to really know Lisbon, Cascais, Estoril and Oeiras and the surrounding neighborhoods. We had many new friends, met every cat, (there are a lot of cats in Oeiras) and felt we were leaving home again! The weather which had been stormy and windy in October and November, (some days bringing in winds of more than 50 knots and sideways rain into the river) had settled into a pattern of cold, but clear and sunny days with light North winds. A good time to head down the coast! Except for a brand new problem.

When we first bought the boat it came with roaches. And it was bad. After two attempts with a small extermination company, we still had a problem. We finally got rid of these awful pests by hiring one of the biggest exterminator in the country, Terminex, who not only bombed the boat, but continued weekly inspections for a whole year. We never had another roach after that. We became religious about avoiding ever getting them again. Under the advice of the exterminators, this meant NO cardboard on the boat, No paper grocery bags, no paper potato sacks, no cardboard egg cartons, no cardboard boxes, and NO CORRIGATED CARDBOARD *EVER*. Then we had the transmission oil leak in Amora. When the mechanics took out the gear box, they laid down a roll of corrugated cardboard to protect our varnished cabin sole. We got to the boat *after* the mechanics rolled out their cardboard and we stared in utter horror. We didn't know how to say "Stop" and it was too late anyway. We hoped beyond hope that it was bug free. But one day before Christmas I noticed a tiny black (really tiny) bug running on the galley counter in the middle of the night. I thought, "Oh, it's so tiny. It's just a little bug." But by the first week in January, the number of tiny bugs grew. They also were bigger And there were indeed roaches. We were infested. We had to hire an exterminator. This meant finding a hotel for us and a place for the cats to go as well for one night. Henrique took the cats to his house and we got a cozy little room at a cheap off season price in a motel right next to the marina. Couldn't get more convenient than this. The room, old but clean, had two single beds that we pushed together, a vinyl covered couch that we covered with blankets when we sat on it, and a coffee table. It also had a tiny kitchenette. And it was cold. Robert, smarter than me, collected extra blankets, pillows and a little electric space heater that we bought earlier (it had the correct European plug) and took it all to the room before the exterminators arrived. With the blankets and heater, and a big pink tree flower that I picked from the tree right in front of the room and put in a beer bottle on the coffee table, our little getaway became cozy.

We noticed that there is very little heat inside many places in Portugal in the winter. And often the doors will be open to indicate they are open for business. The folks in the marina office wore coats inside. We ate at Peter's cafe during the extermination and it was so cold in there I wore a coat, scarf and gloves right up until the food came. Only the gloves came off.

The exterminators guaranteed their work, and would return in three weeks for a check up. Three more weeks! We wanted to be there for the check up. The extermination was not cheap, and we wanted those bugs gone. This roach issue dictated our schedule! Our plan was to leave right after the check up.

CHAPTER 22

Funky Fish Town and Cold Carnival

After a sail with a few new friends to check the new steering arm as well as take our friends out, the day to go had arrived. We fueled up, said our goodbyes, complete with poster signing all around, hugs and kisses. Now free of bugs, we took off on a clear cold morning and motored down the coast to an anchorage off a little town called Troia, in a small protected river. We were headed to a city called Sines, (pronounced "SEEEnish") half way down the coast that had a reputation for being nicely sheltered. The marina there was very reasonable in price. Besides Troia and Sines, the Atlantic coast of Portugal offers zero protection for any kind of anchoring. It's all steep rocky cliffs. It is possible to day trip down the coast if you watch the weather carefully. We arrived to the harbor entrance late afternoon. There wasn't much room to anchor. Where there was room, the water was shallow and the area was crowded with colorful fishing boats. We headed to the marina and were in a slip by 5:00, enough time for a walk into town before dark. The marina was nicely sheltered and we felt safe.

Our trip was under sunny skies, and through calm seas, (motored the whole way) but it was cold! The forecast was for colder weather (below freezing) to come. We arranged to spend at least one week at the marina. The price went down the longer the commitment. Sailing (or motoring) in the ocean in 30 -35 degree weather is just not that much fun. Besides, now we had a new town to see!

Before we left Annapolis, I read about all the possible stops in Portugal, and saw little photos of them in cruising guide books and on the internet. Seeing them in person was a completely different experience. Sines is a beautiful and quaint fishing town with a small but important commercial shipping port. It's a bit industrial at the town's edge, but once inside the small city, we were greeted to more beautiful cobblestone streets, a castle that doubles as a museum honoring Vasca de Gama, ancient buildings mixed with modern ones including a very stunning modern library with a polished stone wall that had only internet access in town. The walk from the boat to the library was short, but most of it was up, and up and up. Sines has some very steep, and very smooth cobblestone streets!

Blog: Extreme Cobblestoning

Feb 6 2012
37:55.98N 08:52.74W

The first time I experienced Extreme Cobblestoning was in Sintra actually. We had climbed up to the top of the mountain by way of paved road and then dirt paths to the Moorish Castle. After the return dirt paths, we decided to go down through the old town. We turned a 900 year old corner and looked down the narrow street, with the cobblestones worn smooth and slick from centuries of use, and shiny enough to reflect the late afternoon sun. I was wearing flip flops, a brand called Urban Beach, similar to Reefs, that had proven to be really fine for lots of walking. But they were seriously wearing out and I was about to learn this. I started down the street, and immediately went into a slide, to which I instinctively responded to by crouching into a deep knee bend and used outstretch arms to balance and hips to steer, and descended with style to a safe landing below. Leg and ankle wise, It was not unlike windsurfing down a wave, except I had no booms to hold onto, or perhaps it was like skateboarding, only I don't skate board, yet.

I chose to take off the flip flops and continue down using barefoot walking as my descending method, mainly due to the thickening hordes of tourists I didn't want to hit while sliding on my worn out shoes.

Soon after this little event, we had to hurry to catch our bus back to Oeiras.

I didn't repeat the cobblestone slide, opting instead to buy new flip flops, for fear of hitting someone while showing off. And after a while, I forgot about it. But I didn't forget about cobblestones.

Portugal has a lot of cobblestones. In the Azores, they are made out of volcanic lava. And mostly dark. But in the towns, the cobblestones were mixed black and light gray, and they were laid out in intricate designs. Often depicting maritime images, historical sayings or just abstract designs. In Cascais, the cobblestones ware also dark and light, although I don't think they are lava, and every where they are, they form patterns. In some cases walking on the wavy patterns makes one dizzy. The streets look like moving water and waves. In Alfama, the neighborhood surrounding Castello St. George in Lisbon, the cobblestones are chunky, and multi versions of dark greys and browns. I could not figure out how the local women could so easily cruise these roads with their spiky high heels that are so rampant here in Portugal.

While we were hunkered down in Oerias, we hoofed every street on the way to either the train station, the store or the old town. There was construction going on at one traffic circle, and quite a bit of new home construction in the newer residential areas. We noticed that the sidewalks around the traffic circle, which had been completely torn up, were replaced with the same little cubes of white cobblestone, and dusted with sand, and therefore easy to walk on. I was quite impressed and relieved that they didn't choose to go with a faster cheaper surface like black top or concrete. The new homes that were being built, were being surrounded with new white cobblestone sidewalks. I even picked up one of the curious stone cubes as a souvenir!

I've been wearing Vans shoes, that are 4 years old and have served me well as comfortable, good looking hip walk around shoes. But the bottoms have seen better days, And they are beginning to wear out. Actually, totally worn out. Back in Annapolis, they showed signs of wearing out when I was painting a giant outdoor mural that had a steep slope of grass in front of the wall. I would try to walk up the hill to get to my work and slide down backwards. I stopped wearing the Vans as work shoes. But here they've been great as walk around shoes. They also have enough thickness to the suede to be warm, and can be worn with fleece socks. It's been one of the coldest Winters ever here. Although sunny and dry, we've been getting very chilly nights well down into the low 30's.

The Vans have become the shoe of choice for walking into and back from town on cold days. Only now they are a bit dangerous, and they slide. However, being that there aren't so many tourists around, I can turn this "danger" into "sport" and start shaping and inventing Extreme Cobblestone Sliding, maybe even turn it into a competitive sport!! Maybe start the First Annual European Mid Atlantic Regional Cobblestone Sliding Event! Maybe I can invent some cool moves and give them names, like the Pivot Jibe in windsurfing, (which I got good at) or the Twizzle in ice dancing. (which I did not get good at, yet)

I really miss working at improving skills involved in a sport. Any sport. I really have been considering taking up skate boarding. They have some really weird and cool looking skate boards around here that look like lots of fun, but probably cost a lot. I also considered inline skates, but again the cost. But I already have the Vans, and the old slick cobblestones are already here and the hills are steep. So if I can figure out a way to gracefully slide down steep historic Portuguese cobblestone hills, knees bent, arms out, hair flying, I'll be sure to name some tricks, when I invent them.

We ended up spending three weeks in Sines and loved every minute. We were visited by the marina's immigration officer, Nuno, on the first night. He was so friendly we wanted him to hang and have a beer. He noticed our Gibraltar stamp, and commented that it was odd that we had a Gibraltar entry stamp as our last stamp, but here we were in Portugal. However, he didn't seem too concerned. The next day, we were feeling awkward about this passport status. We instigated a visit to the immigration office to seek their advice. It was such a unique situation, they really didn't know what to tell us.

But they loved to talk! They were bored, and we were their entertainment. We all agreed that we would document our return to Portugal from Gibraltar by bus, and create a paper folder, and just have it on hand. They didn't seem too worried. They were more interested in talking about water sports. They had read my blog and were all excited about extreme cobblestoning. Clearly they were not worried about us being illegal. Nuno asked Robert for help in repairing his hang gliding sail, which Robert could easily do, and another friendship grew. We felt at home in this place.

Blog: Becoming Locals

Feb 19 2012

Queijo Curado Amanteigado, a local cheese, is 50 cents cheaper at the Spar store than at Pingo Doce, But Pingo Doce has our favorite wine that we call "Scallywag", since we can't pronounce its real name. The Mini Preco has Suma Zero pineapple soda. The Spar and Pingo Doce don't even carry Suma Zero. This is the knowledge of locals. And we now have this knowledge.

We have found ourselves off the beaten tourist path throughout this adventure. Because we look for grocery stores, hardware stores, banks etc, and because we have gotten to know some folks including cashiers in stores, we feel more like locals than tourists. Even in Bermuda, I had a twinge of feeling local when we did laundry in the laundromat and shopped in a sail loft as opposed to the souvenir stores. Twice I was asked if I lived there, in Bermuda. We don't get mistaken for Portuguese, (could be the hair color,) but we are treated like locals and have been asked if we are living here.

I was thinking of calling this adventure, "The Great Grocery Store to Grocery Store Atlantic Tour", and still may. When you aren't rich, you don't eat out. We eat in. And that means going to the grocery store. I don't mean stocking up for Ocean Passage making, but for day to day living. We've seen a few old fashioned markets, but not as many as I would have thought. There was a fairly large Municipal Market in Horta that had various vendors selling vegetables and flowers, but the meat and fish stands were closed when we got there. There was an amazing market in Angra on Terciera, and I stocked up cool vegetables, fruit, and meat. The was a decent market in Seixal, but ONLY Saturday mornings. They had the best cheese, but the worst bread. There are lots of very small groceries everywhere, and they are great for some fruit, cheese, emergency pasta or wine, and they are also usually very friendly. We really liked one small grocery in Seixal, never got the name of the owner but we got to like her and she seemed to enjoy us. She helped us with the language and turned us on to some weird fruit. In general, we enjoyed the character of the markets but they often had such limited hours and when you get around by dinghy and walking, this could mean getting to the market too late.

Larger stores are open all day into the evening. And they all have good prices and excellent food. We find what ever is within walking distance. The chain Pingo

Doce is common here. The name translates literally to "Drop Sweet," and it loosely translates to "Small and Sweet." The Pingo Doce in Lisbon near our marina was the biggest one, (so far) and it was still very small by Grocery Chain standards. The other Pingo Doce stores are squeezed in train stations, mini malls, or small neighborhoods. It's a full grocery store, selling everything, including having a deli, fresh fish, mandatory dried cod fish, meat and plenty of produce, just small. I learned to get used to getting bumped into and waiting my turn to go down aisles. In Oeiras, we got to know all the cashiers, the butcher and the fish ladies. We'll miss them.

The big chains are absolutely humongous. Like the American Giant and Target all in one, with the grocery part even bigger than the Giant. (50 cashiers!! 50!!) These are where we stock up and we usually get a ride or a taxi. Except in Horta, the huge store, a chain called Continente, was close enough to walk to.

The day I felt I really arrived at becoming a local, at least as far as language goes, was not long before Christmas. We were in Cascais and stopped in the mini mall's Pingo Doce before getting on the train. I filled my hand basket with stuff for dinner and got in line. I had figured out that the Pingo Doce cashiers ask every one if they want a plastic bag (sac) and how many (you are charged 2 cents per bag.) Although I couldn't repeat what they say, or write it here (not yet anyway) I knew what they want and could answer in Portuguese. This one day, the cashier first said "Boa tarde" to which I said, "Ola, boa tarde" and then he asked the usual saco question and I replied "Tres" (3) and I also noticed he had many little colorful little candles in tiny jars next to the register, that clearly looked like Christmas candles. So this cashier asked, in Portuguese, if I wanted to purchase one of the candles. I recognized enough key words and knew what he wanted, so I asked "Quanto custa?" (how much does it cost?) and he said "Um Euro" and I said "Sim, um" (pronounced Seeng, oohm) (yes, one) and he asked which color, again I heard the key words "qual" and "cor", and I replied "Azul" because I like blue. Then he told me my total, I paid with exact change, said "Obrigado" and left. I left beaming! I don't think he knew that I didn't really speak Portuguese!!! Well maybe I am now! The grocery stores have so far been the best teachers of this dificil (deeFEESHial) language, as well as the marina staff.

And then here have been occasions of being somewhere and seeing someone we know and it's just like home. I'd be walking down the dock and hear, "Hey Cindy! What's up?" Every now and then I get that song in my head that goes "I think I'm turning Japanese, I think I'm turning Japanese, I really think so," Only I, of course, insert Portuguese instead of Japanese.

I may be turning Portuguese, But I am not going to start taking 2 hour lunches when I get back to work!

We still wanted to make some progress south. We were planning to head out at week two, but the folks at the marina convinced us to stay for Carnival, which is how we ended up staying three weeks. The city of Sines hosts this carnival every year that tries to be of the same scale as the big Carnival in Brazil. They hold it on the same day, and it takes up the whole main street and lasts a few days. The parade was big, colorful and festive featuring floats, loud music, dancers, children, and costumes that included gigantic headgear. Some with feathers, some in the shape of horse heads, and lots of sparkly things. If they could have incorporated live birds, they probably would. But no live birds. Our plan was to get up at 4:00 AM the next morning and head out. We left the party early and hunkered down for the night. It was very, very cold. With the exception of the Carnival's Latin dance beat sounds still coming from all night partying up on the hill, the dark morning was still and quiet. One degree colder, we would have had ice. We silently motored out of the harbor and turned the boat south. We had over 60 miles to go to get to any kind of "safe" anchorage, and wanted to get there before dark.

Blog: Rounding Cape St. Vincent

Feb 21, 2012
36:58.08 N 08:56.55 W

Some call it a milestone, rounding Cape Vincent, aka Cabo de Soa Vincente, when heading south along the Atlantic coast of Europe. It is the lower left corner of Europe, where Portugal's Atlantic coast becomes the Algarve. Cape Vincent, and the next point, Ponta de Sagres, have been referred to as a "formidable pair." Wild and windswept. Sometimes seen for miles, even in Summer. Sometimes heard before seen. What we saw was a big cliff with an old lighthouse on top, and what I heard was Robert putting beers in the fridge.

We have been watching the weather very closely now that we are moving once again. Portugal has been experiencing one of the, if not THE coldest and driest Winter. We haven't seen the infamous Southerly storms since November. And there has been no rain. The winds have been Northerly for the most part, and light. But the air has been cold. So we've been aiming for relatively short day trips so we can avoid sailing in the night, when, many times now, the temperature has gotten down to freezing, literally! Once in Sines, (pronounced SEEnsh, sometimes SEEnish) we needed to plan for a good day to make the 57 mile trip around the cape to this somewhat protected anchorage off Ponta de Sagres. So averaging 6 knots, it's easily a 10 hour day. And another 12 miles to Lagos, the next stop. When we first arrived in Sines, the days barely had 12 hours of daylight, and it was freezing. Literally. The weather forecast was good so we took off this morning at 5:30 AM. Pitch dark and freezing. But calm and quiet. Later the sun warmed things up enough that I didn't need gloves, and what breeze did fill in was from the North so it wasn't in our faces. Even with clear sunny skies, I never took off my coat, over two layers of fleece on top of Under Armor long underwear. (Still wish I had bought Under Armor stock when that company first went public. Oh well.) As we did approach the cape, the breeze filled in nicely and we had a delightful sail around it and into our anchorage.

Besides the weather, we have been monitoring the fuel filter like a hawk. After sitting so long hunkered down in Oeiras, "stuff" may have had a chance to settle in the tank. We have a much loved pressure gauge in the engine room and a good view of the glass bowl on the Fuel Filter. We chose to motor sail to make at least 6 knots, and for most of the day the wind was too light for that. And as the hours clicked by, the dark region of sludge was increasing in the glass bowl. It was like a game, do we keep going at this good speed motor sailing, or turn the engine off, just sail, clean the bowl and lose time? Then the wind filled in to a nice 15 – 20 knots. It's a good thing the wind came because we both heard the slightest change in the engine's "tune," and turned it off before it shut down. Letting it shut down due to lack of fuel could let air into the fuel line, which would mean we'd probably have to bleed it which is a pain in the butt. Although, there was a time that I could bleed a 4 cylinder diesel in less than 8 minutes. I was thinking of starting the East Coast Diesel Bleeding Championships but never got around to it.

Anyway, we had a delightful sail, maintaining a good 6 knots, and we were still able to start the engine to maneuver into our spot and drop anchor. Then we cleaned the gunk out of the bowl and we are good to go tomorrow, but not at dreaded 5:30 AM. It is very odd, however, to be anchored here, with a town right in front of us, up high of the cliff, and wide open Ocean directly behind us. Would not want to be here in a South wind.

It's nice to be on the move and seeing new places!

CHAPTER 23

Jail Gyms and Nervous Nellies

We were officially in the Algarve, the name for the whole southern coast of Portugal. We spent one night anchored in front of Sagres. It is a "cove" of sorts, resembling a "U" on the chart. With the wind out of the North, we were protected by the cliffs, but we set the clock and did an anchor check every two hours all night to be sure conditions hadn't changed. In the morning, the engine would not start! Gunk did settle and caused probably a tiny bubble of air to get into the fuel line, and we had to bleed it. Fifteen minutes later, the anchor was up and we headed to Portimao, 12 miles along the coast and up the river Arade and anchored. In town, at a boatyard, we saw our friends from Horta, Michael and Rhonda, the ones with canvas/sail loft. It was a great reunion and they invited us on a day of touring in Lagos, a nearby town popular with tourists and where they live on their boat, as well a day in the mountains by car. A real treat indeed.

As it was late February. We were getting more concerned about our "Creative Passport Status" and made an appointment to see the immigration officer at the marina in Portimao. We arrived at the marina by dinghy for our appointment. We were directed to the immigration officer's office. There, we handed him our passports and as he inspected them, he expertly twirled a neon green pen around his fingers. I was curious why I cared about this. Then, through the translation of the marina's office manager, Lida, he told us we were very illegal and could go to jail! He was not nice at all about it. We explained, through Lida, that we just wanted to be good people, and that we went to Gibraltar by bus, as recommended by an immigration officer in Cascais. The Portimao officer yelled some more, saying, through translation that it had been the wrong recommendation. We asked if we could get Nuno, the officer in

Sines, on the phone, to explain that we had tried to make things "right" there. Robert had Nuno's number in his speed dial. We think the officer was briefly impressed by this. We heard only the loud end of the conversation. It turns out they know each other. Finally, after the phone call, the officer (he carries a gun I might mention) said, through Lida, that we could take another bus trip to Gibraltar and get a second stamp. That this would "even out the stamps."

We inquired about Gibraltar bus trips in town and got some good information. The marina let us do laundry and use internet in the office even though we were anchored out. While online we noticed a perfect weather opportunity to sail the 120 mile trip to Gibraltar over night. Moderate winds were predicted from the west for over 48 hours. Not a common weather pattern this time of year. We decided to just go to Gibraltar by boat. We brought the boat into the marina for one night to water up, fuel up, and get ready for the overnight trip.

While in the office lobby, where I was tapping away on the computer, the immigration officer came in and I said "Hello sir! Hello!" (I was very nervous around him.) "Look here," I continued, pointing to the weather map on the marina's lobby bulletin board. "The wind is coming from the west, (like he cares). So we are going to go to Gibraltar by boat, and we are here now for one night to get fuel and water and wash the decks and get ready for the trip which is 120 miles, oh wait, you guys use kilometers, so it's, let me think...."

As I kept jabbering he interrupted me and spat "Get your Passport!" (in somewhat English). My breathing stopped! Oh no! We're going to jail! I hope they have a gym in jail! I ran down to the boat, passing Robert on the way and said, completely out of breath from fear, "Passports. We need our passports."

Back in the office, we nervously handed over our passports to the officer, and to our surprise, he stamped them! A Portugal stamp! Good for another 90 days! Just like that! Then he simply turned away and went about his daily business.

We called Nuno, and explained the whole puzzling event. Nuno explained that when our boat was anchored out, the Portimao officer didn't have to deal with us, legally. But once we were a marina customer, he had to deal with us, and to stamp the passports was simply the easiest thing for him to do. This, plus the fact that the first day we had seen him was "before lunch" and he was cranky because hadn't had his "beverage" yet. The second day was *after* lunch. Got it. This was cause for a celebratory beverage of our own!

CHAPTER 24

One River, Three Towns

Now that we were good and legal in Portugal for the next 90 days, we did not sail to Gibraltar the next day. Instead, we moved to a city owned marina that we discovered when walking around. This marina, located in the heart of the town of Portimao, only charged 10 euros a night, including electricity and water, but had a three night limit. 10 Euros! Such a deal! We thought it would be fun to be right in the middle of town. The Portimao marina, although nice, is a long dusty walk into town. Our plan was to spend three nights downtown and then anchor out.

We headed to the downtown spot. The current at the city marina is wicked strong, but I managed a perfect landing. Had I noticed the white water rapids circling the pilings, I might not have made such a good landing. The strong current caused much strain on the spring line on the boat behind us, and was enough to rip the cleat right out of the dock. Good thing we were there! We retied that boat so it wouldn't bang into us. Then we notified the marina manager, Huey, who didn't seem to know what to do about the cleat. I guess you get what you pay for!

After our three days, we decided to try and anchor in front of the town of Ferragudo, across the river from Portimao. Although our previous anchorage inside the jetty was close to Portimao Marina and had good holding, it was a long dinghy ride to town. Not only did this mean a lot of gas being used to dinghy back and forth, but when we did go into town, we felt so far away from the boat. It's a very disconcerting feeling, like part of you is with the boat. We wanted to get in closer. As soon as we had the anchor down in front of Ferragudo, a guy on his boat on a mooring warned us the holding was not good. He was Nick, and he suggested we ask at a restaurant, called Sueste, right in front of the sea wall steps, if we could use an available mooring. The mooring was owned by the restaurant's owner. Nick seemed pretty sure he'd let us use it.

The sea wall steps are concrete, steep and slimy at low tide. But they are the only option for landing a dinghy in Ferrgudo. If they are not slimy, they will be, and plenty of line will be needed to secure the dinghy as the tide goes out. We needed to make sure the dinghy wouldn't be in the way of other boats using the steps as the tide comes in, so we used a large iron cleat about 10 feet from the top step. We were standing with the line in our hands, about to tie up, when a local man said "Here, this is good." He took our line and secured to the iron cleat. Then, pointing, he said, in beautiful English, "Are you on that beautiful American boat out there?" We said yes. He said "Why don't you use my mooring? It's the red ball in front of where you are anchored. I won't need it for a couple of months!"

This was the guy Nick was talking about! We were going to look for him and he beat us to it! He introduced himself as Amadeau, and he insisted on no payment for the mooring. We made a mental note to patronize his restaurant for a dinner. The least we could do.

Knowing how limited the anchorages are along the rocky coast of Portugal, this mooring spot right in front of Ferragudo was a good find! The coast becomes more sandy as it goes east towards Spain, but still, there are few sheltered harbors. Like realtors say, "Location location, location." We were in a really good place to get to know of some of the flavor of southern Portugal.

Ferragudo is a very small and charming fishing village. It has many steep narrow cobblestone streets, bright colored doors inset into white washed buildings, a friendly town square, small shops and restaurants, cafes and lots of cats. A beach called Praia Grande, that runs along the mouth of the river and looks out to the jetty, and beyond to the Atlantic is a short walk from the sea wall. This beach is at the bottom of dramatic golden cliffs and some of the cliffs over the past thousands of years have "dumped" some of their "rocks" and as a result, there are large rocky formations right down on the beach that you can walk on top of and under, through cavernous holes. There is also a striking castle right next to the edge of town, built in the 15th century to protect Ferragudo from pirates, and is now privately owned. Must be nice. We loved walking to the beach and climbing over and hiking under these golden rocks.

We could still dinghy over to the Portimao marina and walk to Praia de Roche. Praia de Roche is hopping in the summertime when thousands of Europeans descend here for sun, fun, and beach time. But this was still February and it was quiet. The main street of Praia de Roche runs along the top of a long cliff, and is comprised of huge classy hotels, casinos, lively nightlife, old smaller hotels, lots of shops and restaurants. Most shops were open and many waiting for summer. Lush green tree lined zigzagged walkways made their way down to the beach, which has soft white sand and more steep sun kissed golden cliffs.

We could also take the dinghy to a free dock at the Sardine Museum in the heart of Portimao, where we were docked for three nights. Portimao is a sizable city which had a lot of activity in spite of still being winter. This is where the grocery store was. It was a Pingo Doce! It was a short walk from the dinghy dock at the sardine museum, which made our Ferragudo mooring location perfect. Ferragudo only had very small grocery stores with limited hours. Although these small stores were cute and friendly, the Pingo Doce became our primary source for daily meals. Remember, this is the Great Grocery Store to Grocery Store Atlantic Ocean Tour.

We visited more with Michael and Rhonda. Robert even borrowed some table space in their loft to lay out a template for our new sail covers, that he planned to sew on board. I did some more painting. Since leaving Oeiras, I got into a new routine of setting up a painting space inside the boat, and painted under a hung work lamp. In Sines it was too cold to paint outside. As it warmed up, and when it wasn't too windy, I'd paint outside in the cockpit. I had a body of work growing, and another show coming up back in

Annapolis. I tried to make time for painting as often as I could. I grew to love painting sessions, listening to American radio on the computer (when we got internet) and having an ancient European town right outside. Heaven!

One day, we decided to go into Portimao and look for a framer. We found one, and to our surprise, his door was open after 1:00, and before 3:00. He was open during lunch! Unheard of! (except shipyards). Inside we met Antonio and his wife Sun. And we asked about his open hours. He told us he lived and worked for a few years in a country whose traditional lunch time was only 45 minutes, and he realized he liked this better than a huge filling meal in the middle of the day and chose to stay open. He also felt more productive and saw business improve.

A two hour lunch is a long solid tradition in Portugal, and it is a big deal, as well as a big meal. Sometimes it is a four or five course feast. No wonder it's hard to return to work. Things are changing, slowly, though, as Portugal becomes more used to a market economy. Still, if you say you don't eat lunch, they look at you funny.

Antonio took the paintings to frame. We talked with him and Sun for over an hour. While we were there, he had a visit from a South African woman, Gayle, who had moved to Portugal 30 years earlier to raise a family here. She told us her story.

"It's so safe here," she told us. "I could take my kids in the woods and sleep on the ground if we wanted to, with no worries, not even a snake." We later were invited to visit Gayle at her Finca, (farm) where she and her husband raised short designer palm trees for landscaping. Portugal was getting more appealing by the day!

We solidly enjoyed our stay on the mooring while we got to know the town, the people, the beaches, caves and caverns around Ferragudo, Portimao and Praia de Roche. The weather started to get warmer, and the time came to continue along the coast.

CHAPTER 25

Glitz Parade and Jumping Puppies

There are a lot of places to stop along Portugal's southern coast. Each one is unique. And the port that was closest to where we were is called Villamoura. Villamoura is not a town, it is a ritzy marina village, and a major tourist destination for Northern Europeans. The marina is the largest in Portugal and probably the fanciest. It is surrounded by high end hotels, restaurants and golf courses. There is a long beach that continues to a small old town called Quateira. There is a constant parade of well dressed people walking from one end of the marina complex to the other. Women in Gucci pants and Prada shoes join men in colorful golf attire along the promenade. Cafes serving colorful cocktails with techno lounge music playing, line the waterfront. Shops selling expensive designer jeans and jeweled bikinis, are joined by souvenir stands and jewelry stores. Not the kind of atmosphere we were seeking, but there was an alternative reason to go to Villamoura. We had learned back in Oeiras that there is a year round ice skating rink a few miles from this marina. So we got a slip! Then found a taxi, and once again we had a chance to ice skate in Portugal. In spite of the glitz we really liked Villamoura.

The marina was still in "Low Season" which meant the prices were still affordable. We decided to buy a week, which brought the price down more. The week went by fast. Our neighbors were friendly, the marina was well protected from surf, and the slips were big and easy to get in and out. The marina has a well stocked chandlery and two grocery stores were very close. The walk along the beach to and from Quartiera, an authentic old town, was delightful. We also could walk through residential neighborhoods to get to Quartiera. It's funny how certain experiences stick in your head. One evening we were walking back to the boat from Quartiera and we saw two dogs in a fenced in yard. One was a large shepherd mix and the other a small yappy dog. They would bark intermittently. The shepherd would say "Woof" and the yapper would say "yap yap." Again "Woof" followed by "Yap yap". It sounded like: "Woof yap yap Woof yap yap Woof yap yap" and so on. The woof yap yap was Funny enough, but what we saw was priceless. The shepherd stayed rooted on all fours while the yapper literally jumped up five feet into the air, completely vertically and perfectly timed to the Woof yap yap beat. Up on "Woof" back down for his yap yap. It was a golden moment that had us laughing so hard we couldn't walk. If these two dogs could take this show on the road their owners would be seriously rich.

CHAPTER 26

Cultures of Water, Sand and Fish

Our next port was in a region called Ria Formosa which includes a popular island called Culatra, a rather large city called Faro, and a small fishing town called Olhao. (pronounced OL yowl) The surrounding wetlands are rich in sea life, and fragile as well. It is extremely tidal and tricky to navigate. We started out anchoring off of Culatra. Many cruisers claim this to be "paradise." It is a small island with an old fishing village on it. The village is a throwback to a much older time. They just got electricity for the first time in the late 1990's. There are no paved roads, just sandy ones, and people who live there commute to the mainland by either ferry or their own boats. We learned that the anchorage gets very crowded in the summer season. But the day we arrived was still in April, and only one other boat was anchored. The wind was blowing a solid 20 knots. with higher gusts. Although the water was flat, it didn't feel protected enough to hang out there. We chose to head to the town of Olhoa, which has a reputation as a more protected place to anchor.

We dropped the hook right in front of the town, after waiting for the tide to come up enough to make it there. One piece of advice we had received back in Villamoura was to wait until mid tide. At mid tide, the marsh is visible on either side of the channel. High tide covers the marsh enough to give an appearance of wide open water. Even though the channel is marked, the current is swift, and seeing an actual marsh makes navigating this area much easier. Once anchored, we felt we were in a good spot. We learned that we could tie up our dinghy at the end of a very long floating fishing pier. We went into town and checked out Olhao. It's a small city, no where near as touristy as Lagos or Praia de Roche. Much more real than Villamoura, and had an intoxicating charm. Many of the buildings were covered with intricate colored tile that along with the cobblestone streets provided architectural eye candy. The waterfront promenade was a park that was grassy and landscaped, and in the middle of this park were two red brick buildings, kind of odd in Portugal, that have large busy markets inside. One is mostly produce, and the other seafood. The markets and the waterfront are a tourist attraction. One day we saw a bus load of camera clicking northern Europeans all get off the bus, walk to the water's edge, snap away at the pretty boat anchored (*Tenacity*), and get back on the bus. Besides this occasional tourist frenzy the town seemed quite genuine and we decided to stay for a while and get to know the place.

Besides instant attraction, another reason we wanted to stay at this anchorage was we had friends from back home flying to Madrid. Their plan was to rent a car and explore southern Spain and Portugal, and then meet up with us where ever we were. Olhao was a good looking town off the beaten tourist path, that had old Portugal flavor and some history. The island of Culatra was an easy ferry ride away. We decided this was a good spot to meet our American friends, Laura, Doug and their kids Alyssa and Rob. They were to arrive in a few days. This gave us time to find a place for them to stay. After a bit of asking around, we found a great funky old guest house right in the heart of town. It was a local cop who steered us to this perfect find.

The thing about Portugal and cops is that not long ago Portugal was a strict police state. They haven't known freedom for that long. This has many affects on the behavior of the people and the general culture today. One of things we noticed is the number of uniformed police. Just 30 years ago all these police had a big job and a lot to do, making sure the people were "in line." People couldn't talk freely about the government back then without possibly getting into trouble with the law. But now, the police are bored. There is very little crime and traffic flows OK. People pretty much obey stop signs (unlike America) and as a result, there is an abundance of police standing around, smoking cigarettes and shooting the breeze. When we walked up and asked a group of cops for their advice on a place for our friends to stay, they practically pushed each other out of the way to be the one to talk to us! I am not making this up.

We had discussed taking our friends sailing but the tide logistics for their day were not very good, it would mean that we would have to head out practically before dawn so we scrapped that idea and instead decided to take a ferry and visit the funky island of Culatra. They arrived by car in the evening early enough to enjoy seeing the guest house and meeting its owner, and then we all had a typical Portuguese dinner of grilled fish and potatoes at a waterfront restaurant. We planned on catching a morning ferry to Culatra.

The ferry ride was actually a bit bumpy! It was blowing a solid 30 knots, and it was cold! I was glad that I had advised Laura and Doug to bring warm clothes. It does get cold in southern Portugal! Culatra did prove to be funky and charming. No cars at all. Just a tractor or two off the side of the village. We saw one church, a little school, and small cottages and cafes lining the main sandy road. We walked towards the other side of the island that faces south into the Atlantic. On the way we came to a lagoon, that has a small opening and a somewhat large but shallow bay. Only boats with shallow draft can come in and anchor here. It has become known among cruisers and many have have ventured in, mostly catamarans, and some have planted their roots here and have stayed for decades! In fact, some of the boats no longer resemble boats anymore. They are beached and have become surrounded by makeshift awning structures, grills, lawn chairs and gardens. We later learned that these folks are now claiming property rights and there are fist fights over who has what "land." Seems like squatting to me.

After lunch in a village cafe, we all headed back to Olhao, and they headed on to their next stop. Although it was a short visit, it was wonderful to have friends from home actually experience a bit of what we were doing and we were happy to show them a few fun sights that may not have been included in their Portuguese Travel Guide.

Our next person to meet was our friend Orlando in Faro, just a few miles away. Orlando lived in Annapolis back in the 80's and hung with the same boat folks as us. We knew him, he knew us and we know many of the same people all from Annapolis. And there we were, on his turf!

He came to meet us and invited us to his house for a few dinners. Orlando is one of the most talented cooks I have ever met. Dinners at his house were the best food experiences of this adventure. People often ask us about food, assuming we eat out a lot, which we do not. But we did a little, and hands down, Orlando's dinners were the best. He even gave us a "tour" of the fish market, where there were some of the weirdest looking sea creatures I could imagine. He picked up one of these creatures and showed it to us. I thought, "uh oh, I may be eating barnacles tonight." I saw a wiggly looking slimy creature that looked like a foot of a three toed wet sloth, and Orlando said "THIS looks delicious!" Ew. But once he was finished cooking these weirdo slimy things, they were mouth watering delicious! I had seconds and thirds.

Our visits with Orlando and his wonderful family were such a highlight. He drove us around and helped us with the language, gave us a tour of Faro, took us to a wine tasting. Portuguese wine is some of the best wine we've ever had. It was nice to have a friend nearby.

We felt very much at home in Olhao. Our walkabouts took us to every part of the city. A huge nature park that showcased the Ria Formosa, and its history was also nearby. We even found a do it yourself Laundromat and became regulars there. I discovered a piano in a café and played well enough to be applauded by the patrons. The place had a welcoming nature and we loved it.

But it was time to finally move on.

CHAPTER 27

New Country!

Next stop Spain! We motored out of the Ria Formosa and headed east towards Ayamonte. That day we had light wind, and pretty much motor sailed to make decent time. It was a delightful trip, but we had to keep a watchful eye out for fishing buoys. We had heard of another sailor who wrapped her prop around a fishing net and the buoy was partially submerged. She was alone and had to dive in still cold water to cut the line off the prop. This did not sound like fun. We watched for signs of buoys.

Ayamonte is a delightful city at the mouth of the Guadiana River, the river that separates Spain from Portugal. Across the river is the Portuguese city Ville Real de St. Antonio, often just called Ville Real. Both have really good reputations as places to see but Ville Real has a famous wicked current. Several other cruisers discouraged us from trying to get into that marina. A boat can anchor here in the river, but it's busy with commercial traffic, strong currents and a ferry crossing back and forth all day. The better anchorages are quite a way up the river. We opted to spend some time at the marina in Ayamonte. Again, it was still low season, and buying a week was better than by the day.

Right away we could tell we were not in Portugal anymore. The language sounds completely different. Of course. The music in the grocery stores was very Spanish. A lot of salsa music. In Portugal we'd hear their pop music as well as American pop music in stores. I liked the salsa music. I immediately noticed that salsa music does not require auto tuning.

There were all kinds of different foods that we never saw in Portugal. We saw weird fruits and veggies, bumpy melons and twisted squash. There were canned and jarred foods like olives stuffed with anchovies, or jarred broccoli and asparagus that was so overcooked it was almost yellow. These were all over the shelves here but not in Portugal and Portugal was barely a stone's throw across the river! There were different kind of sea creatures in the seafood section. Even the smells along the streets were new.

We learned that instead of a two – three hour lunch, they take a three– five hour siesta. They actually go home, physically put on their pajamas and go to bed. This meant stores are closed from 1:00 to 5:00! And when they open back up, they stay open until 9:00 PM. Starting about 5:00, the town squares fill up with families of many generations, little kids right along with their grand parents, playing, shopping, eating, and relaxing. The atmosphere was so welcoming. We were liking this place!

We bought a couple of weeks at the discounted price. The weather was warming up and we both got into the spirit of working on the boat. Back in Oeiras, there had been a couple of warm days and we did some chores. One chore that I started was to take out some of the wood trim that is inside the head, and scrub it clean, sand and varnish. Now I decided to start the outside woodwork, which consisted of the rubrail, hand rails and deck chocks, which may have once been used for a dinghy but now they are just there. They don't leak, so instead of taking them off and risking deck damage, I have been keeping them varnished. I didn't get time to do it before we left Annapolis and as a result, the varnish was peeling and looking rather sad. Well, very sad. We had brought along plenty of supplies for this kind of work. There was also a rather well stocked and English owned chandlery a short walk away. Being English owned meant they stayed open all day, knowing cruisers don't break for lunch or siesta if a boat job needs to be done. So I started with the paint and varnish remover that we had, and began the job of stripping off the old varnish. Some say the definition of cruising is doing boat maintenance in exotic places. Very true!

Robert took on the job of cleaning the water line, since now the water was warm enough to swim. In fact, the weather warmed up fast and became hot! We got into a routine of morning exercise, coffee, market or grocery store, then work on the boat and walk about town in the evening. Or get right to boat work and save the walkabout and store for later. We got a lot done. One day, I was sanding the rubrail was getting tired. This was not like me! I was used to working long hours. Then I realized it was after 9:00 PM and the sun was still bright! I was thinking it was only about 6:00! I had been at it since 9:00 that morning and got completely fooled by the sun being so bright so late!

Back in 1988 I bought a little hand held sander made by Ryobi. It still worked like a champ. If it stopped working, we fixed it. Well, it stopped working on the second day of sanding. Robert took it apart and discovered the brush inside needed to be replaced. This was going to be challenge in Spain, since we speak limited Spanish, and no "Rapid Spanish" which is the main language here. We took our little sander into town, starting at the English Chandlery. Then worked our way from one hardware store to the next, trying to explain what we needed. We actually were understood and we ended up at a tool store that had Ryobi products. I think the proprietor was impressed at the age of our sander and that we were trying to fix it instead of replacing it. Also, he appreciated our efforts at speaking his language. He had the part, and he and Robert worked together, sometimes speaking two different languages and got it going again. Then we went back to the boat and continued our projects.

In spite of doing so much work on the boat, we still got to see and really enjoy the town of Ayamonte. We took a day off of boat work and took the ferry to Ville Real. We went walking every evening. Our walkabouts revealed a city rich in architecture, colors, town squares, and a little public park with zoo animals! Lions, zebras, a bear, a tiger, goats, ducks, deer and exotic birds, just a block from our boat in a small grassy park. We learned from a fellow cruiser that the city "adopted" retired circus animals and created this public zoo/park, and it was free. It appeared that the animals were very well taken care of.

One day we discovered that there was a veterinarian right across the marina parking lot. We realized our cats were due for their annual shots. This was so convenient that we made an appointment for a check up. When we brought the cats in for the exam, the woman at the desk asked for our passports. We looked at her puzzled. She said, "Oh! You're Americans! I forgot. You don't have pet passports in the U.S.. Would you like Spanish passports?" Our eyes grew huge!

Of COURSE we would! What better souvenirs could we get than official Spanish pet passports, complete with photos of our cats! Their exam went great and they became official Spanish kitties all in one afternoon.

The woman who was the veterinarian's assistant asked about our trip while the cats had their check up. We told her all about it, and the conversation segued into what we did for work. Robert told her he was a sailmaker and I explained I was a free lance artist. Now her eyes grew big. She asked what kind of art, I explained I did all kinds of stuff, lettering, portraits, murals, and she stopped me at the word murals.

"I want a mural in my house" she told me. "I had asked an artist friend to come and look over a year ago and never saw him again"

"I'll do it!" I said. We made arrangements to go see her apartment after she got off work, (9:30, still bright and sunny) and we came up with a plan and a budget. I did some sketches and she gave me a key and I painted two very nice murals in her apartment. I made some money, and decent money at that! Wow! This gave me "International Muralist" status. The decision to go to that veterinarian proved to be great one.

CHAPTER 28

One River, Two Countries

The folks in the marina office strongly encouraged us to go up the Guadiana River. "Not to be missed" they said! But they also asked how high our mast was. There is a suspension bridge that boats have to go under to get up the river, and it is rather low. So low in fact, its nickname is the "X Lax" bridge since it looks like you will surely hit it as you go under. Not all boats can go under. The bridge height at low tide is barely 70 feet. We planned to go on up the river and timed our trip with the tide. We also told the marina that we'd be back and they offered to give us the discounted price when we got back even if we didn't stay more than a few days. Nice people.

Our cruise up the river was spectacular after the finger biting tenseness of going under that bridge! We swore we were going to hit but we didn't. We motored up the winding long narrow river and eventually arrived at a popular destination for many cruisers. We dropped anchor in the middle of the river, with the town of Alcoutem on the Portugal side and San Lucar on the Spanish side. We were about to experience the Guadiana Glue!

Blog: Guadiana River

May 21 2012
37:28.29N 07:28.25W

20 miles upriver from Ayamonte is a gem of a place that is unique, friendly, beautiful and full of history.

The river has a wicked current, sharp bends and eye popping scenery. The further up you go, the higher the hills on either side, becoming mountainous. Virtually no development exists except a few quintas (Portuguese farm houses) and a few fincas (Spanish farm houses) sprinkled in among the sloping grass and trees, and also an occasional tiny village on the Portugal side. You might see an occasional cow and some sheep. The sounds of many song birds are impossible to ignore, as is the sound of sheep bells as they are being herded by actual shepherds. The color of the water becomes what they say here, "chocolate" as you get more inland.

The river separates the rival countries Portugal and Spain. Seemingly at war with each other throughout history and somewhat still today. Going up, Portugal is on the left, Spain on the right. And there is a one hour time difference. Portugal sides with the same time zone as England, one of their closest allies, while Spain sides with the same time zone as the rest of Europe.

Once you reach the two towns of Alcoutem on the Portugal side, and San Lucar on the Spanish side, the "Guadiana Glue" starts to take hold.

We arrived in the very late afternoon, and after a healthy long anchor watch in 20 –25 knots of wind, we ventured into San Lucar Spain to look for a pay phone, thinking that the later hour in Spain would make for a better time to call the U.S., not realizing that it didn't matter. We landed our dinghy at the free "pontoon," as they call it, which is a floating pier parallel to the sea wall. It is free, and some of the boats have been tied to it for many years. We walked into "town" which hosted a café, a bank, and a closed tourist office. Which we later discovered never opens. I couldn't get my eyes off the incredibly beautiful planted flowers on most of the porches of the spotless clean apartments, and the luminous pink glow, casted onto the white building sides, reflected from the red floor tiles of their porches.

But the town was oddly quiet. We found a teeny tiny grocery store and asked (in Spanish) if they knew where the pay phone is. The guy inside answered (in Spanish) and we walked right to it.

The next morning, we went into Alcoutem and discovered a much more lively place. Busy cafes, little shops, tourists, (not too many) a hardware store, museum, bank and a tourist office that was open. Also we talked to several folks on their boats, tied to the "pontoon" (10 Euros a night with a "relaxed" 3 night limit).

The time it takes to dinghy from Portugal to Spain is seconds, not minutes, and by the end of the morning, we had staked out all three grocery stores (tiny) two in Spain, and one in Portugal. The Portugal one has better bread and frozen meat, and the Spanish stores have better fruits and vegetables and general stuff.

Later the second evening we had a knock on our hull from a man standing in a flat sided dinghy.

"Hello there, welcome to the Guadiana" said our new friend Paul, from Ireland. "Do you plan on staying a while?'' he said after introducing himself. We told him we planned only to be there a few days, because we have crew flying into Faro soon, and we needed to start the trek back towards West.

"Well I'd like to invite you to a sort of Happy Hour at the Seaside Tavern in Alcoutem tomorrow evening. All the boat people go. Starting around 8:00, Portugal time!" He then proceeded to tell us about some great trails not to be missed for hiking, including one that involves possibly meeting Paco, an 83 year old Spaniard, full of history and stories, who rides one of his 2 donkeys out to his finca from town and back every day.

So the next morning, we did go into the Spanish side and hiked the trail along the river, and came to a spot where we heard the unmistakable sound of a donkey and shortly after, saw a little guy leading two donkeys toward a little stone wall, supposedly built by Romans a bunch of years ago.

We asked him if he was Paco, and he answered "Si! SoyesterytuioPacocbertalladauioretyuislestlcbatyuattala ttabatladdaladalatta!!!" (Rapid Spanish)

If we had understood Rapid Spanish, we could have learned much about Paco and his family and the history of San Lucar, but we do not speak Rapid Spanish, and instead we nodded and smiled, and had a wonderful hike up the stone road (laid by Romans).

Later, we did go to the Happy "Hour" (which for some was more like Happy Many Hours) and saw our friend Marcell who we met in Portimao. We also met many new boat folks. Marcell was sad when we said we weren't going to stay that long, because he wanted to hire me to paint eyes on his boat. (he pronounced eyes "Hise, with an H and hard S) So I said that I could do it the next day, which I did. And on the way to his boat, by dinghy, people waved to us from their anchored boats, and shouted, "Are you on your way to paint Marcell's eyes?". Word gets out fast!!

The job was tough, from the dinghy, in 28 knots of wind and a 3 knot current. But I finished. However I wanted to return the next day to do a second coat. Which I did hanging upside down, once Marcell removed some netting, which made the job MUCH easier, given the same 20 plus knot wind was still causing the dinghy to pitch and roll. I talked him into a shadow on the already painted name, and he was so excited he tipped me 25 Euros and offered to take us out to dinner!! I like this place!!

We also met another Paul, from England, who has been there several years living on his boat. He had found a little shack to rent, and get off his boat, that you can only get to by dinghy if you went by water, Or maybe donkey, if you tried by land. There was no road leading to the shack. Paul invited us to come and see his new shack and we went by dinghy. We sat on his new porch and swapped sea stories and boatyard stories. I love this place!!

The next day Robert and I were on the san Lucar side and we saw a dog walk by and stop in front of us. I tried to make friends with this dog but she just stared passed me, and then we heard the clanking bells and thunderous footsteps of thousands of pounds of fluffy wooly sheep barreling down the steep hill behind us. The dog was a working dog, and herding these sheep was her job, and she was busy. It was rush hour in San Lucar!

The fact that so many cruisers never leave here is referred to as the "Guadiana Glue" and I totally get it. I can see how attractive it is to stay, with the beautiful river, cozy grocery stores, winding walking paths, colorful flowers, tons of sheep and such friendly people. There is even a fresh water beach on a little creek on the Alcoutem side that is wonderful. It would have been so easy to stay put.

But we have to move on. We headed back to Ayamonte.

CHAPTER 29

Coastal Slop and New Crew

It was approaching June and once again our passport stamp's 90 day time limit was coming to an end. We made an appointment with the immigration office in Faro, and went by ferry from Ayamonte, and then took a train to Faro. This time we got very nice folks. They looked at all our paper work, our new bank account, and proof of health insurance. They even let me take the time to brush my hair and put on lipstick for the photo. $180 later we had an extension good until end of August. It felt good being legal. We even met Orlando for a beer before we headed back to Ayamonte!

A couple of days earlier, we had received an e-mail from Alan. He convinced us to return to the Azores by boat, and to visit his island for all the spring festivals that are held there. He would be our "local friend" AND he was available to help us sail there in early June. It was now late May, so we needed to make a plan. Returning to the Azores sounded wonderful. Alan made arrangements to fly into Faro. This made heading back to Ayamonte and then west along the coast towards Faro the first time we actually back tracked this whole adventure, which officially started the journey home. I was very sad to be leaving my new friends in mainland Europe. But I looked forward to the sailing that we had ahead.

After saying our goodbyes in Ayamonte, we headed out the river and west along the coast. On this day the wind was light and we were motoring. Our destination was either back to Olhao, or Culatra. There were large swells coming from the south so the motion was uncomfortable but we still made good time. The breeze filled in later also from the south. And as we approached the entrance to the Ria Formosa we saw a military style boat, similar in size and shape as a PT boat, leaving and it was thrashing through waves becoming almost airborne before smacking down onto the water. It's forward motion was very slow. We looked through binoculars and saw huge breaking waves entering the passage. This was not an ideal situation to be going in such a narrow entrance with rocks on either side. When we entered before, the wind direction was from the northwest and the entrance was fairly flat. Not this time. We continued west to Villamoura. The marina entrance there was man made and had long sea walls deflecting the swells that made entering easy. Then, after a couple of nights there, we headed to Albufiera where we were to meet Alan and his buddy Richard who would be joining us as crew.

The 5 mile trip to Albufiera was a 3 hour event. The wind forecast was light, but it kicked up to 25 knots. right as we were leaving Villamoura. Classic. We figured we only had 5 miles to go so off we went. The swells were still out there and this big fresh breeze this time was out of the southwest. It became a slow wet ride, into sloppy 6 – 8 ft waves. We couldn't logically sail because the wind was smack on our nose, meaning we would either have to sail into the beach or head out to sea, tack and head back. We could have done that but, well, it was only 5 miles and we were lazy. The scary part was heading into the marina's entrance. First we entered a small bay, which drastically reduced the waves, but then we needed to go through a fairly long and very skinny passage with concrete walls on either side. The tide was low so it felt like being in a coffin, and 25 kt wind just made it nerve racking. But once through, the marina proved to be one of the most protected marinas in all of Portugal! And they brag about it! Since we had gotten a late start, it was almost dark when we arrived, wet and tired from our arduous 5 mile journey. After we checked in at the office, we relaxed and chilled and enjoyed a seafood dinner, saving our walkabout for the next day.

Albufiera is a hugely popular beach resort for northern Europeans. The marina was a short walk from the main town. In town we found an old cobblestone infested beachy place with hundreds of shops selling bright colored plastic beach toys, rafts, buckets, bracelets, bathing suits, flip flops, sunglasses, woven bracelets, scarves, sundresses, metal bracelets, shell jewelry, shell bracelets, shells, tacky stuff made in Taiwan, more woven bracelets, sunscreen, leather bracelets, fancy shoes, designer purses, beaded bracelets, incense, watches, more woven bracelets, towels, umbrellas, and bracelets. Something about wrist adornments was very important there. In spite of the tacky shops, we really liked Albufiera. (You may have figured out by now we liked every place we went.) The town was old, intricate, and had lots of character and the beach was accompanied by huge dramatic golden cliffs, bigger than Praia de Roche!

We also found the two large grocery stores that we would need to patronize for our 900 mile voyage back to Terciera.

Robert and I celebrated our 24th wedding anniversary there and chose a restaurant right in front of the boat for our dinner out. We met another couple at the restaurant who was celebrating their 40th anniversary! Same day! We also ran into a cruiser who we met in Portimao. It was like old home week. The next day Alan and Richard arrived. We enjoyed having Alan back and were getting to know Richard. We had "met" him on the phone months back when Alan had called to say happy birthday. It was back then that he started to plant the seed about returning to the Azores. We were easy to convince, we knew we loved the Azores, and Alan told us about the many festivals they have in the spring and early summer, and we became excited about seeing Terciera again.

We spent couple of days in Albufiera, giving Alan and Richard time to see the town and the beach while we got the boat ready for sea. Robert was busy making sure all the systems were working fine. He spent much of the time maintaining everything, so things were already in good working order. I worked more on the varnish and got the cabin comfortable for our new crew. Robert's constant maintenance was a huge reason our trip was so enjoyable on so many levels. When we, mostly Robert, invest so much time taking care of the boat, we believe the boat will return the favor and take care of us. We had our share of boat issues back before we left. But once off the coast, this boat has proven to be safe. Maybe this is one reason why Alan felt comfortable enough to return for another multiple hundred mile journey.

Robert was satisfied with all the systems and gear. We all went to the grocery store and loaded up a taxi with groceries for 4 people and a week at sea. The plan was to get up early and head out. We were leaving mainland Europe!

CHAPTER 30

Up and Down and Slow and Steady

The forecast was OK. Winds would be out of the Northwest starting at 10 − 15, building to 15 − 20, building again to 20 − 25. The wind direction looked as if would be NW for the next 10 days. Probably longer. Only the velocity was supposed to change, and increase. It would be a one tack beat, pretty much the whole way. Otherwise it looked fine, sunny, clear with no low pressure systems lurking about. *Tenacity* is good sailing to weather, or upwind, but it can be slow. The wind was very light at dawn the morning we left. We said goodbye to a gorgeous Portuguese coast that sparkled in the early morning sun and motored out into the Atlantic. By afternoon we were sailing. By evening it was windy. Everything was fine except Alan and Richard were getting seasick. I made a very simple rice and beef dinner which they seemed to keep down.

Richard had been having a difficult time adjusting to reading the wind direction meter and would turn the boat into the wind, thinking he was turning away, and as a result, he'd accidentally tack the main, or stop the boat. He got upset with himself, and Robert told him it was a common error and he'd get the hang of it soon.

Then the steering stopped working. Oh no! After all the checking and rechecking! Robert decided to heave to (adjust the sails to "sit still") and went to check under the bunk and saw that the tiller had slipped down it's shaft, the stop key had dropped out, probably from vibrating over time. Thankfully the stop key was right there easy to reach. It was an easy fix and something we couldn't have predicted.

With the steering up and working, we stayed hove to for the night to let Alan and Richard get some sleep in the hopes they would feel better. By dawn, we were off again but Alan and Richard were feeling worse. This was becoming worrisome. We had heard stories about seasickness and knew it could be deadly. We tried to encourage them to drink water. They were able to hold watch, but it was clear they were getting sicker.

The next day the steering stopped again! Same thing! So once again we hove to, and Robert and I went back together to deal with the slipped tiller. Robert wanted to replace the bolt that was holding the tiller clamp together but it was too stubborn to simply come out. So he cut it off with a hacksaw. Then he replaced it with a new one that had a lock washer, and I suggested putting hose clamps on the shaft under the clamp to prevent it from slipping down again. Success! This is still holding today and shows no signs of budging.

We were back in business. But Alan and Richard were getting weaker by the hour. Thing is, it was not that rough. It was actually kind of nice! The wind was a steady 20, the waves were about 5 feet, the skies were bright blue and sunny with white puffy clouds. The sailing motion was slow, up and down, but manageable. What worried us was if this was bad enough for our guys to be sick, what would happen when the wind increases as it was supposed to do? With two chunks of time spent hove to, we still had a long way to go. If our guys became unable to hold watch that would leave Robert and me. And if something happens again, like the steering, we'd be exhausted. Which was not the only issue, what if Richard and Alan got so sick that their health was in jeopardy? We were not used to being faced with this kind of situation. I wanted to love being out there, and I did to an extent. I looked around and saw the beautiful surging seas and endless sky and knew our boat was strong. I had faith in Robert in his leadership, and being able to deal with things like the steering clamp. But I found that I was really sad. Probably because our crew was not enjoying this. We were sailing along, up, down, slow and steady, the steering was working now, the engine was fine, the boat strong, the sun bright, but our crew had become basically unhappy cargo. I made a simple pasta dinner that Robert and I ate. Richard and Alan were able to eat a little, but were clearly miserable. Then, Robert announced that he made a decision. We were going to change course and head to Madeira.

The thing about the open ocean, there is no "road" with guard rails or lanes. You can turn away from waves and wind if crew is really sick, or if the boat is taking a beating. It's actually so simple.

Not long after we turned south and eased the sails, I saw color returning to Richard's face. Richard confessed he prayed that we would change course! Alan didn't argue. Robert entered the new course to the island of Porto Santo into the chart plotter and instead of beating into the wind and waves, we were now surfing! I was a bit disappointed about not returning to the Azores, but relieved to see our crew come back to life. What a difference a course change makes! The guys were eating, talking, discussing politics, and even enjoying the steering. Richard especially! I was so happy! I figured it was a good time to write another MOTO Gazette blog!

MOTO GAZETTE
Middle Of The Ocean Gazette

Eastern Edition

Headline News

North Atlantic Ocean has Been Returned after Upgrades and Repairs

The eastern section of the North Atlantic Ocean, mainly south of latitude 38, and north of latitude 30, and east of longitude 30, known for it's choppy high seas and often unpredictable weather, has been returned to it's original place after an extensive 6 month overhaul.

Beginning last September, 2011, a group of Ocean activists, known as the North Atlantic Improvement Association, (NAIA), comprised of cruisers, yacht racers, fisherman, and delivery captains, banned together and lobbied for this section of the Atlantic Ocean to have a complete makeover, to make usage more user friendly for small craft. Financed by the E.U, The United

States, and Fillipe, the NOIA worked with oceanographers, marine scientists, meteorologists and magicians, to create gentler breezes, calmer seas and less salt.

"Have you ever tried washing all this salt out of your yoga pants?" says Cindy Fletcher Holden, co-owner of American Yacht "*Tenacity*", who completed a successful transatlantic sail summer of 2011.

Some worry the reduction of salt will affect the salt pans that are still active in the Ria Formosa outside of Faro Portugal. "If these people take away my salt," Says salt pan farmer, Henrique Rodriquez, "it may hurt my living!"

But scientists assure Mr. Rodriquez and other salt pan operators that there will still be plenty of salt to pan. "Probably people could stand to eat less salt anyway" says Fletcher Holden, also an active member of the NAIA.

Now that the North Atlantic is back in service and open once again to sailors and mariners alike, it's difficult to say for sure if the improvements really worked.

"It sure is fun when you're on a broad reach!" Says Alan Venn, crew on *Tenacity*.

Time will tell if the overhaul took hold. Meanwhile, ships, fishermen and sailors are back on the high seas, hopefully enjoying some good June sunshine and gentle 25 knot Northerly winds.

Business News

Tenacity Sea Products introduce New Products for 2012

EverDamp, the successful air spray from Tenacity Sea Products, that allows the armchair sailor to truly experience life at sea, now comes in 3 new aromas just in time for the summer season, "Low Tide, Spilled Diesel, and Last Week's Ravioli." Also new this year are InstaWet, and AllSalt. InstaWet allows you to experience wonderful sensations such as a cold wave plopping on your head from behind. It can be installed anywhere in your home and can be set to go at random. AllSalt can by plugged into any outlet and within minutes, there will be a slick salty coating on surrounding surface within 50 ft.

Tenacity Sea Products is working hard to make life on land as close to life at Sea!

Sports News

North Atlantic Fitness Center to Host 2012 Eastern Atlantic Cockpit Wave Riding Championships

The North Atlantic Fitness Center, which opened last summer, will be the official host of this year's challenging Cockpit Wave Riding Championships. A sport that combines the athletic prowess of a stunt horseback rider, the delicate balance of a dancer, and good working electronics. The idea is to achieve the highest average speed while sailing down waves on a broad reach. There will be divisions based on boat size. In the 14-15 Meter Division, Cindy Fletcher Holder is entering with her yacht "Tenacity."

"It is such a thrill!" She says, "I not only look at the actual speed, but our GPS displays how much time there is until the next destination. When I hit that sweet spot and blast down a good wave, I see the destination time drastically reduced! My goal is to arrive by yesterday!!"

Some say Fletcher Holden has had too much time on her hands to think clearly, but we at MOTO Gazette are pulling for her and Tenacity to achieve high points at this fun filled event!!!

Legal News

Lawmakers Lobby for Better Boating

After years of studies, and miles of seafaring, the International Association of Maritime Lawmakers, IAML, whoever they are, have created a new law which, starting July 1, 2012, will make it unlawful for sailors to sail to weather, also known as beating, in the North Atlantic. There will be exemptions, for example, a yacht actively racing will be exempt from this law. The IAML has also laid parameters to which this new law will be enforced. Called the "Beat Index," this number is achieved when adding the wind velocity in knots, to the wave height in meters. So if the wind is 25 knots, and the waves are 3 meters, the Beat Index is 28. The IAML has set the minimum allowed beat index to 25, so a yacht beating in 28 of more, will be subject to fines beginning at 500 Euros. Other exceptions will include if the yacht has less than 80 miles to go to its destination, and if the crew is "happy."

This new law goes into effect right after an extensive over haul of the North Atlantic that allegedly assures sailors, fishermen, ships and seafarers calmer seas, gentler winds, and less salt.

Citizens Pissed at Empty Toilet Paper Rolls

For decades, perhaps centuries, it has been a common practice to "pack paper" when traveling, or even just walking around Europe. Public and private restrooms, also known as "WC's," never seem to have any toilet paper. Even in some of the finer restaurants, you'll find a modern, clean, decorated restroom, complete with attractive paper holder, but no paper. Recently a number of angry citizens banned together and formed the European Alliance of People with Tiny Bladders, EAPTB, and are asking lawmakers to create a fine for establishments who do not have paper in the restrooms.

"How difficult is it to just have some rolls of paper there" asks Beatrice Foster, from London, living in Albufeira Portugal, "The only time I found paper in the restroom was in a café that was owned and run by a woman." But men are fed up as well. "I don't get the logic" says Paul Keester, from Holland, living in Portimao, Portugal "They have the fancy roll containers, but no paper."

The EAPTB hopes to have the new law in effect by this Summer, in time for the high tourist season in southern Europe.

Letters to the editor

North Atlantic Over Haul

Dear MOTO Gazette

Last week my wife and I sailed from Morocco to the Bay of Biscay, in rough seas and Northerly winds never below 25 knots. The waves were 3 – 6 meters and our boat took quite a beating. This was after the "North Atlantic Overhaul" which promised us smoother conditions. We fear this is another example of the EU flittering money away at useless projects with no logic in sight. What are they going to pay for next, a Supermarket and shopping mall in the middle of the ocean? Considering their record of spending, this would not surprise us in the least.

Roger and Mary Rose Sears, Brussels

Lost Hat

Dear MOTO Gazette

I dropped my favorite hat in the Ocean at N 32:42.59 and W 17:10.17, if any one sees it please contact me at 351 915 253 999. It is a white cotton hat that looks exactly like the one that Gillian wore in the TV show, Gilligan's Island. Thank you very much.

Bob Denver, United States

Ocean News

Shopping Center Coming To The New North Atlantic

Soon, sailors and fishermen alike will be able to stock up or grab a few groceries, and have a coffee or a beer while passage making in the newly overhauled North Atlantic Ocean. Sponsored by the EU, the shopping center will include a Continente Grocery store, a Sports Zone sporting goods store, Modelfa clothes and accessories, Worton computer and music store, Vodo phone, shoes, book store and a cinema. The mall will be air conditioned and have several cafes and restaurants. A welcome break from long distance sailing or fishing expeditions, this shopping center should be a success by all standards. "What a delightful addition to the new Ocean!!" says Pedro Silves, director of the North Atlantic Shopping Center project, "We hope to be up and running by July, 2012."

In addition to the mall, the EU plans to build a full service marina adjacent to the shopping center, complete with a boatyard, chandlery, launderette and internet. Boats can tie up for just a few hours while shopping, or rent a slip for a longer period of time to relax and enjoy the break. There is also talk of apartments and offices included in the mall project.

Obituaries

Skip Squid
June 12 2012

Skip Squid died suddenly while attempting to leap over a sailing yacht in the newly overhauled North Atlantic Ocean. He crashed into the cabin top, and never saw the Sea again. Mr. Squid's father, died in a similar fashion just a year ago in the same waters. Mr. Squid is survived by his wife, Slip.

Services will be held at happy hour in the cockpit.

CHAPTER 31

Surfing to a Big Brown Rock

The winds, as promised, increased to 20 – 25. The waves built to 9 to 12 feet and we had a blast sailing down them. In this much more comfortable motion, I cooked up some good dinners and we were all able to enjoy the ride. Robert or I checked on the steering every few hours, and although the tiller slipped a tiny bit, it was holding and holding strong.

We ran the engine to keep the batteries topped off but just for an hour a day. We had the new issue of the shaft being tied off with a shoestring to keep it from spinning. Robert would go below and untie the shoelace that was keeping the shaft from turning, and then we turned on the engine. After one hour, we'd stop the engine and Robert would go back into the engine room, and yell "OK HEAD UP" which later became a simple "OK" which meant for us to head the boat up into the wind and stall, on purpose, so Robert could tie the shoelace back on. Then we'd hear "OK, Fall Off" and we'd get back on course. This became a routine that would last the rest of the journey!

Just before dawn on June 14, we spotted the Madeiran island of Porto Santo. Richard was on watch. He said, very quietly, "land ho." To which we all slept right through. Robert got up for his watch and saw the big brown island and said, "Richard! Next time say it louder!" This has since become a running joke. Every time we made landfall from this day on, we would quietly say "land ho." Then do all the alerting and what ever it takes to get folks up.

CHAPTER 32

Rocky Cliffs and Steep Prices

We called the marina in Porto Santo (the only marina) and let them know we were on our way in. They had us tie up at the end of a long floating dock. Easy landing. We checked in with the officials and headed into the small but charming town to check things out. That night, we celebrated dry land and safe landfall with a dinner and a movie. On board! While we were inside the dark cabin watching "Oceans 11," Alan raised his glass and said, "Now THIS is yachting!"

Porto Santo is one of two islands in Madeira that are inhabited. Porto Santo is quite barren, brown and rocky. It is rather beautiful in spite the lack of green. It is barely developed, with just one town, that is mostly sandy beach. It's a popular spot for tourists, especially tourists from the island of Madeira seeking sun and surf. Most of Madeira's coast is rocky and steep. We met a fellow sailor, Roger, a retired radio news producer from the UK, who offered to give us a tour of the island with his car. We were able to see the whole island in a matter of a few hours. Robert and I could have easily stayed right there for a period of time, but there were a couple of things keeping us from doing that. One, Alan and Richard needed to get to the island of Madeira to catch a flight to Terciera, and the other was the marina was outrageously expensive. The only anchoring option was right off the beach which had no protection at all from the south. So after a few days in sunny Porto Santo, we sailed the 22 miles to the island of Madeira.

CHAPTER 33

Green Valleys, Orange Roofs, Boatyard Jets and Rock and Roll

Four hours later we were tied up at one of the most over priced marinas we have ever seen, and again, no option of a safe place to anchor. Called "Quinta do Lorde," the marina is part of an unfinished resort community. The marina/resort is on the eastern most point of Madeira and the driest part. The surrounding cliffs are dramatic and beautiful. The marina staff was friendly and helpful. The docks are well built with decent power and water, but besides the office, nice docks, laundry room, bulldozers and mud, there is nothing to offer. They wanted to charge almost 100 Euros a night! ($130) and no weekly or monthly discount. It would have been great at a third of the price. We nicknamed it "Quinta No Resorta." The nearest town was three miles away and it had no grocery store. The marina provides a van that goes to the next town that does have a grocery store, ten miles away. Then they expect you to take an expensive bus back. Most of the slips were empty. No surprise! When we were in Porto Santo, we got to know Norman in the marina office and he raved about Quinta do Lorde. He also suggested they might be interested in a mural. I brought up the idea of doing a mural to the Quinta No Resorta staff. There was enough interest for me to do a sketch. I even offered to barter slip fees for work. But when the idea got to the actual owners, they said no. So we left after two nights.

We learned from fellow cruisers later that this Quinta do Lorde place, the Porto Santo Marina AND the ferry that runs between the two islands are all owned by two brothers, who people use the word "greedy" to describe (they said it first.) It is worth noting that, the ferry schedule is timed so it arrives in Funchal, Madeira (the capital city) from Porto Santo AFTER all flights leave, forcing customers who are traveling to book a hotel in Funchal, and the closest hotel to the ferry is ALSO is owned by the Greedy Brothers.

When Robert was dealing with the slipped tiller (still holding great), he noticed the stuffing box around the rudder shaft was still leaking. It has always leaked a little. We don't own a large enough wrench to tighten it, and we have been on the look out to buy one but they are incredibly rare. Every opportunity we had to borrow one we would. We borrowed one back in Albufiera and had success. But once again, it was leaking. It's not a leak that will sink the boat. It's just an annoying little thing. But annoying enough for Robert and I to consider having the boat hauled for a quick peak to make sure the actual stuffing didn't need to be replaced.

We learned of a boatyard only a few miles from Quinta No Resorta, and decided to check it out. Alan and Richard wanted to rent a car for a day and see the island. Instead of joining them all day, we hitched a ride to the boatyard. This boatyard is hands down the weirdest boatyard on planet Earth. It is UNDER the airport runway. The runway, supported by enormous concrete pilings, causes the boatyard area to feel dark and inside. The sounds of jets taking off were thunderous and nerve racking. Boats appeared tiny sitting under the huge concrete ceiling.

Once we got over the surreal surroundings, we went into the boatyard office and explained we would like to have the boat hauled just long enough to inspect the rudder. We didn't even need a whole hour. They said they had a mechanic who, if needed, could replace the stuffing. The yard manager told us he'd be there at 9:30 the next morning. Well, we would need to leave the marina, which also meant turning in the gate keys (four of them) which had $25 deposits, each, on them. And the office opens at 9:00, and closes at 6:00. We needed the keys to get past the locked dock gate, and back in, the evening before. Richard and Alan were still out with their rental car and we were doing laundry that wasn't done by 6:00. This meant returning the keys before 6:00 was just not going to happen.

166

The boatyard is three miles from the marina. So at six knots, we could in theory be there by 9:30 assuming we were on our way at 9:00, and traveling at six knots. But this didn't give us time to return the keys. We asked if we could make it 10:00. The manager said "9:30."

We said, "10:00 would be so much easier." We tried, again, to explain the logic. The guy said "9:30." (I don't think he was understanding us.) After much back and fourth discussion with no success in changing the time, we decided to at least try. The next morning, we had the lines untied, engine on, and were ready to go at 8:30. At the second the office opened we returned the keys, got our $100 deposit back and took off. As soon as we got away from the protection of the marina's seawall things changed. Greeting us like a happy puppy was 35 knots of wind right on the nose! This is the ocean. So the wind was big and the waves big. Even with the engine cranked up to 3500 rpm, we were barcly making three knots! The boatyard people could SEE this! We could see the boatyard so they must have been able to see us pushing ahead, in the 35 kt headwind. It does not take a rocket scientist to know this kind of wind will slow you down. But they were not rocket scientists, not even close.

We finally made it, at 10:30, and entering that haulout slip was one of the most miserable boat handling experiences I've ever had. It was a sharp 90 degree turn, making the headwind go right to our side, and the high walled concrete slip was hardly inches wider than our boat. I was driving. Robert was handling lines and fenders. My teeth were clamped so hard I'm surprised I didn't do dental damage. My heart was pounding and my hands shaking. But we did it. We were safely in the travel straps scratch free.

THEN the yard manager had the nerve to say "I told you 9:30." ????

I said "didn't you SEE us coming? We were going as fast as this boat could go! Look at the conditions!"

And he said "I told you 9:30." Like a broken record. My blood pressure soared. He was charging us by the hour, and a lot by the hour, for all his guys, starting at 9:30. By the time we were hauled, it was close to 11:00. We didn't get blocked or washed, just stayed in the travel lift slings. The mechanic, named Soloman, and Robert inspected the rudder from the bottom. I stared out to sea trying to will the wind to calm down. All I could think of was getting OUT of that concrete coffin of a haul out slip in this wind. I did manage to go around and look at our bottom. Considering how long it had been since a haulout, the boat looked great. And the stuffing was completely in tact. The rudder looked just fine. It was time to go back in the water. We were out a total of 50 minutes. Robert went in to settle up. The guy kept saying he had to charge us for that early hour of the Soloman's time, as well as his actual time (40 minutes). Plus the haul out, and the yard's time as well. This meant we were charged for all those guys to stand around and watch us plow through 35 knots of wind and six foot waves for an hour and a half. The actual time physically helping us tie up, hauling out and going back in was maybe one hour at most. But they had their clock starting at 9:30 and ticking, for each guy, right to when we were done. The bill came to over 700 euros, which is nearly $900. After some pleading he finally came to a more reasonable price. He kept saying to Robert, "I'm just a working man." Robert replied that he was a working man too, just taking a break from work.

We have since heard from other sailors that it is not uncommon for businesses to over charge cruisers. People often assume that since we are cruising around on a "yacht" that we are wealthy. However quite often the opposite is the truth! Granted, our boat is stunning to look at and looks very expensive. Many cruisers are getting by like us, on a shoestring budget with no income! A few are wealthy, but most are not, and we found this excessive charging brutally unfair but I can kind of see how the judgment is made.

Alan and Richard got a taxi from the boatyard and went off to the airport (right upstairs) and we went back in the water. With helping hands, and pounding heart, I backed *Tenacity* out of the concrete coffin and back into the still persistent and building 35 knot winds, and now bigger sloppy waves. We went just a mile east and into a small bay in front of the town of Machico. We were protected there from the wind, but had a bit of swell coming in. Still, it was a relief to be somewhat safe and know that the stuffing box leak was merely annoying and not a threat. We spent the whole next day anchored there, it was so windy and rough we didn't want to venture to our next destination, Funchal, so we hunkered down and rocked back and fourth. Alot! The swell caused Tenacity to rock side to side nearly gunwale to gunwale. For the first time in my life I actually felt a little seasick! And we were anchored! The winds built, and shifted, we even moved across our little bay to a more protected spot since the wind direction had changed. We were holding well. The rocking was so severe we couldn't even put the dinghy in the water, for fear of banging up the outboard engine trying to put it on the bouncing dinghy. So we just hung there. By morning the wind settled down to a mere 20 knots from the east. Anchored up, we had a nice downwind ride to the city of Funchal. We already had scoped it out by car with Alan and Richard and knew that we could anchor in a "designated" area, and for a deposit of $10, we could get a key and use the marina showers and dinghy dock. The marina was expensive, and full. The anchorage was OK. The holding was good, which is important, but the swell caused more side to side rocking. Not as bad as Mochico however. In Funchal, the rocking was bad, but manageable. We put the dinghy in the water, attached the engine, and proceeded to explore the city.

Funchal is huge! Not huge like Lisbon, but it is a big city with lots of character. It has a lot of history going back to before the twelfth century. The area along the waterfront is teaming with tourists, mostly northern Europeans, and the surrounding buildings are a complete mix of ancient stone, classic European and glassy modern. Some of the hills are steep steep. We were in for a real walking treat! No subway, but there were buses, cars, runners and tourists.

The first night in Funchal was very rolly. As I was making dinner, we noticed fireworks. Big ones, the kind you'd see on July 4th. I put dinner on hold and went outside, held on tight as we rocked side to side and we were treated to a massive and spectacular display of intensely colored fireworks. The next day we found out what this was about. Funchal boasts having the biggest fireworks display in the whole world on New Years Eve. Pyrotechnics come from all over the world to get the bid for the show. Funchal hosts a competition every summer starting in June and running four weeks. The competitors put on their shows on four consecutive Saturday evenings. I don't know how the city narrows it down to four but we saw week number three that night and it was amazing. We knew we had one more night of fireworks to go!

The next day was not as rolly, as the swells from all that wind were dying down. We continued to explore the city. We found the grocery stores right away. We went on walkabouts in every direction. I found a few running routes.

On day three, we were approached by the Port Authority to pay for anchoring. The manager in the marina office told us someone would be coming by so we were not surprised. This had nothing to do with checking in with immigration, it was just a way to collect money. The official, in an inflatable, gave us two forms to fill out with our name, the boat's name, the boat's length, (they charged by length, which makes no sense anchoring) and where we were from, where the boat was from, etc. Then we kept a copy and the guy kept a copy. He said it was 5.16 Euros a day. (who came up with this number?) One week came out to 36.12 Euros ($52). We handed him money and, pointing, he said "Oh no, you must pay over there at the Port Authority Office." OK, fine. We asked if we could go by dinghy, and he said "No, you must walk around." I knew from one of my running routes that this Port Authority Office was over a mile around the harbor. I was already annoyed, because I don't believe anyone should be charged for dropping an anchor. Also I was still fuming from the boatyard, but I kept my mouth shut. Later we walked the mile and a quarter around the harbor, in the direct sun, to the Port Authority office. Inside, we explained to the receptionist that we were there to pay the anchoring fee. She had absolutely not a clue what we were talking about. And she spoke English. She took

Robert to another office. But not me! "Only you, sir." Weird. I waited in the lobby and listened to the receptionist tell me all about the New Years Eve Fireworks show. Then Robert came out shaking his head. He told me the lady in the back also had no clue, and that Robert explained about the officer who came to our boat, and the forms (of course we left our copy on the boat) and finally she came up with a new paper bill, and said our total for the week would come to 102.57 Euros. What???? Robert explained this was not the same amount we were told. FINALLY she found the copy and we paid our 36.12. Later, we met a few other cruisers who were anchored and each one had their own story, no two boats charged alike. We ended up staying over three weeks and never set foot in that office again.

We did however get to know the folks at the marina. We grew to really enjoy Virginia, the manager, and Sergio, the dockmaster. Virginia was so friendly to us, helping us with directions to places, the language and whatever we needed. Sergio was also helpful and friendly always stopping to chat. To this day Virginia and I still chat and have even sent gifts back and fourth.

One hot day we met a couple on their boat as we dinghied into the marina. They were Brian and Dorothy and we instantly bonded. They invited us on board for a cold drink, and gave us a "tour" of our Canary Island cruising guide book, since we were planning on going there next. We could tell we'd be seeing these two more.

Later that same evening, we were out on the boat, getting ready for dinner and Robert went to run the engine to top off the batteries. The engine ran fine but the alternator was not putting out any charge. Not good. It was getting dark, so the solar panels wouldn't be of any use, and the winds had gone totally light. Robert was worried that the batteries wouldn't last through the night with the freezer still going. We decided to take the boat into the marina, and tied up along side a work boat owned by the city. We had met one of this boat's crew earlier that day. The security guy on duty said we would be OK. We proceeded to have a good dinner after all. With power at the dock.

The next morning we called Soloman, the mechanic at the evil boatyard. It turns out he had sympathy for us. He heard about the over charging and felt bad. He and Robert actually bonded a bit while talking about the rudder. Soloman said he'd stop by that day, knowing the marina would be charging us full price every day even though we were rafted up to another boat. This was very good news because it was Saturday. We were charged a full day for Friday even though we pulled in after 9:00 in the evening. Oh well. Soloman showed up shortly after we called him. Our alternator was fried, and needed to be rebuilt. Brian and Dorothy saw us and came over to inquire. They had empathy for us, it's something cruisers just don't like to have happen. But this happens. They insisted we join them that night for dinner. We bonded even more with them. Soloman had us all fixed up by early Monday and back to the anchorage we went. Soloman only charged 300 Euros, which this time sounded fair, since he rebuilt the alternator, taking it off and putting it back on, and also came up with a new regulator since our old one was also not working. He had many hours in this job and did not over charge. Even though we were now out another 300 Euros, at least the job was done and done fair! Had we had a spare, it might have saved us some labor, but alternators cost more than $450. One way or another, the money was going to be gone. We were back in the anchorage by Monday evening and enjoying a good charge from the alternator.

CHAPTER 34

Didn't know About Vertigo!

Brian and Dorothy invited us on a "Levada Walk." Back in the 15th century, the Madeiran people began an extensive project to bring water from the top of the mountain to little villages below. (The water there, by the way, is really good.) People hand dug canals called levadas. Over time, many of these levadas have been finished off with smooth concrete, and are still the main way for water to get to towns. Also, over the past many decades, these levadas have become hiking destinations for tourists from all over the world. Some of the hikes are "black diamond level" that involve some serious rock climbing skills, and others are "blue level" that are simply wonderful walks in the forests!

Brian and Dorothy took us on one that we could do in an easy afternoon. We took a bus to a little town called Monte, and started there.

"Are you OK with heights?" they asked.

I said "I've been on scaffolding and up in cherry pickers, and as long as I can touch something I'm fine." Ha ha ha ha. We hiked along some beautiful trails and came to a dirt path fairly high up. The levada was on our left and the drop off on the right. For a while, there was a good bit of ground to the right of the path so it was easy. But the path got skinnier and skinnier. The wall of mountain, on the left of the levada was over a four feet reach, so I couldn't simply "hold onto the rocky mountain side." The levada is about three feet deep, so, yes, I could have gone into the water and still be able to "walk" in waist deep water. The path narrowed to about eight inches wide. To the right was a three thousand foot drop. Three thousand feet! I froze! I could not move! I didn't know if I was crying or laughing, but I was shaking and my eyes were watering. I tried to get down on the knees and couldn't even do that. Brian was behind me, Dorothy was in front. Robert was behind Brian. They were all fine. Brian came up and took hold of my belt, and I held Dorothy's hand and took itty bitty steps until we were past this part, maybe about 100 feet. Then I took a deep breath and we stopped for lunch. I will never forget that feeling. The experience deepened the bond with our new friends. We hung with them for a few days before they headed out to sail to the Canary Islands. Before they left, they gave us a gift, a little walking guide book of Madeira. We used it and went on other levada walks on our own, some even higher and longer, but these paths had handrails and these rails made all the difference.

Blog: Nature Hikes and Walking Trails

July 2012
32:41.30N 16:53.58W

There are abundant nature hikes and walking trails throughout the island of Madeira. There are surprisingly some very nice ones as well in the city of Funchal, the capital city on the southern coast of this green volcanic island.

As in the inner island walks, these also vary in the degree of difficulty. For the sake of simplicity, I'll refer to the starting point as the Marina Funchal, which is situated in the city center and a good place to begin any of the walks.

My three favorites are the Pingo Doce Grocery Store Walking Trails. These are The Dolce Vita Pingo Doce, the Anadia Pingo Doce and the Estrada Monumental Pingo Doce, this last one being the most difficult.

The Dolce Vito Trail is the easiest. It is a flat start, with a short climb about two blocks, but along a shady park, then another two blocks fairly flat to the Dolce Vita Pingo Doce. Once inside, you will find several escalators making uphill climbs much easier. The Anadia Pingo Doce is about twice as far as the Dolce Vita, but a little flatter. However, this walk takes you through some congested tourist areas, where at first you will be bombarded with restaurant hosts trying to lure you in to their establishment, or later hordes of shoppers dodging one another. Be careful to cross streets either in crosswalks (called "zebras" here) or when the light shows a green man. Drivers do not appreciate people crossing in the middle or against the light. Once inside, you almost always find this one packed as it is in more of a working class neighborhood. Beware of people bumping from behind and little old ladies butting in line, Very common here.

The third and most difficult trail is the Estrada Monumental Pingo Doce, nicknamed "Beach Pingo Doce." There are two options to begin this trail. One is to walk along the harbor's waterfront boulevard, which is wide and flat, but then reaches a somewhat short but very steep hill, or to walk along a longer less steep hill that takes you along another park and past the Casino. Once up, you have a decent flat wide sidewalk for about a quarter of a mile along Estrada Monumental, but it can get quite crowded with tourists, some who move wickedly slow and tend to meander from side to side. Once at the turn, you go down a considerably steep hill that takes you along sea front hotels, apartments, and what they are calling "Aparthotels." Towards the bottom of this hill is a somewhat beachy and small shopping center, (although there is no actual "beach" here, it just looks as if there is one) and in this shopping center, over looking the sea, is the Pingo Doce. Once inside here, you will find happy sun soaked people looking for postcards, sunscreen, wine, beer, a drink called "Poncha," and groceries. The atmosphere is generally happy here and quite relaxed. Once back outside, you must go back up the short, but very steep hill. However, once at the top, the walk home is easy.

Funchal offers some rather nice nature trails as well as hikes. Again, starting from the marina, the most popular one will take you along the waterfront to the right, with the ocean on your right, the city on the left. Walk about an eighth of a mile, and this takes to you to a public beach, that is more volcanic rocks, and cement than sand, but it has all the elements of a beach. Sunbathers, swimmers, colorful plastic toys, and plenty of nature, but there should be some warning here as some of the "nature" is inappropriately worn thongs or speedos.

Another nature trail is simply to walk around the seawall of the marina, where you can view plenty of nature about on the boats, some of which are boat owners, and some are paying customers going out to go dolphin and whale watching. Again, some of these natures also are inappropriately attired in thongs, speedos, and high heeled shoes that do not belong on tour boats.

There are a few excellent nature hikes where instead of seeing, you can enjoy the sounds of nature. My favorite is Frog Bridge. You can either wind your way through the west part of the old town, or walk along the waterfront to what used to be two rivers. There is still some water that flows In and out, but a lot of it has been grown over with much grass and moss. There are a few little bridges that cross over these rivers, and one bridge is fairly low, old and arched. If you stand on this bridge, and listen carefully (Sunday is best with fewer cars) you will hear the most enchanting sounds of frogs "talking." There are more than one sound coming from these frogs. One sound is a "eeyooun eeyooun" and another is like a quick chirp. And if you look closely you can see them! MANY frogs!! And if the car traffic is really light, the frogs can be REALLY loud!!!

The other interesting nature sound is actually right above the marina, in front of a little wooden a-frame hut, where a lady stands in front and blows into little ceramic jugs full of water creating a "tweet tweet tweetaleealee" sound. For a mere 5 euros, you can have your own tweetalee jug!

I hope this guide is helpful to anyone who wants to visit the beautiful island of Madeira and plans to spend some time in the city of Funchal.

CHAPTER 35

Fun in Funchal

Funchal is a wonderful city. It truly is. But the rolly anchorage got old fast. It seemed like every third day it was rolly. The anchorage was open to the south, and we did get some southerly breezes but not enough to worry about. At least not while we were there. We read in the cruising guide that if a big blow comes from the south, the marina will take in boats, even if they are full, and figure where to put them, somehow. We were protected from the north, which is the prevailing wind, and as we learned it can go west or east, and if the wind is from these directions the anchorage is still protected. The swells however work their way in and the boat just rocks insanely side to side. It was in a way worse than open sea because we weren't moving forward. We couldn't dare put a glass down without it going flying. We kept everything secured down just like we did offshore.

One day we took a bus quite a way inland to a levada walk. And on the way back, the bus rode along the coast, and we saw enormous white caps, and what looked like a huge southerly wind. We sat in the bus absolutely terrified that the south wind had kicked up (this was not in the forecast) and that our boat could be subjected to dragging ashore. We are very good and careful at setting anchor. But still, seeing what appeared to be 30 knots of wind and six ft waves made us sit on the bus and sweat bullets. FINALLY we arrived back in Funchal. The one hour bus ride felt like an eternity. We ran to the dinghy dock. At this point, the anchorage looked calm. All that wind was "out there," and had enough east in it to keep the wind from coming into the anchorage. But it looked so fooling as we rode along the coast, before the coast bends around to Funchal. From the bus, we saw the wind and waves were pounding right onshore. In Funchal, we were OK.

During our three weeks there, we got to know the layout of the city quite well. We found all the hardware stores, and an electrical store which we frequented to buy fuses. The owner heard us attempt to speak Portuguese and then whenever we went in that store, he only spoke Portuguese, even though he spoke flawless English. He saw and smiled and said "No English anymore! We will speak Portuguese!" I must admit, it was a rush to speak in a new language and be understood!

While at the anchorage, we still ran the engine every day, even though the solar panels and wind generator produced quite of bit of juice. We ran it to keep the batteries topped off as well as heat water for showers. The alternator was working. This was the same routine of charging that we had gotten used to back at other anchorages. But now something was drawing 3.5 amps, and it seemed to be constant. Robert checked everything. At one point, he disconnected every single electrical item in the whole boat and there was still this mystery draw. We feared it was something like an old 12 volt fan that the previous owner had installed in some oddball locker and maybe it had turned on somehow. Robert started to suspect the new regulator that Solomon installed with the generator. He removed it and the draw went away. What was happening was, when the engine was on, the regulator made sure the right amount of charge went into the batteries and it was doing this job just fine. But as soon as the engine was turned off, the regulator got all confused and was looking for something to charge, and kept on going. Now we had a new routine. We manually turned the alternator on and then started the engine, and as soon as the engine was off, we turned the alternator off. It did not take long for this to become habit. The funny thing is when talking about this to other cruisers, we found it's quite common! "Oh yeah" we'd hear frequently, "We just start and stop the alternator manually!"

On one Sunday afternoon, we were walking over a foot bridge, that crosses over what used to be a river, and is now sort of a creek at high tide, and rocks, moss and grass at low tide. There are a lot of frogs down there. During the week, with all the traffic, you can't hear the frogs. But on this Sunday we heard a lot. We had heard the same kind of frog back in Porto Santo under a similar kind of bridge, and we acknowledged how "cute" the sound was, but here the sound was loud. Clearly there were bunches of frogs in that grass. We stopped and looked down. If we looked hard enough we could see them. Lots of them. We heard "Eeeyoo. Eeeyoo." I called back "eeeyoo." Silence. Then I said again "Eeyoo, Eeyoo" and then we heard "Eeyoo eeyoo eeyoo eeyoo" like they were excited to have someone from "up there" talk back to them. I realized after several minutes of this exchange that I was having a "conversation" with the frogs. I may not speak very good Portuguese yet but, man, I was nailing Frog! After another 10 minutes, we noticed a little old lady staring at us. I swear I saw her twirl her finger around her ear as if saying "crazy." Maybe she did, but I loved those little frogs!

We stopped at a small cafe one hot day for a cold drink. I ordered a Cola Zero with ice, Robert ordered a beer. The waitress brought the drinks, along with a plate of food. We said "No, we didn't order that." She said "It's OK, it's free. Gratis." It was a little sampler plate of whatever dish they were serving that day. On this day it was marinated, and pickled tuna bites with onions and crackers. Really good! And just enough for a taste of some traditional food. Also our Cola Zero and beer only came to two Euros! This little cafe was off the beaten bath on a small ancient cobble stoned alley and did not cater to tourists. We ended up visiting this place often and became locals there. They knew what we wanted and when they saw us heading for a table, they brought it out along with the little plate of treats. I even asked about the ingredients and names of the dishes and tried to make them at home. (Still do.) We'd often see the owner at one of the tables playing cards with the locals. Before we left Funchal, we made sure to go and say goodbye to our favorite cafe folks. They had told us earlier that its name was "Cafe Express" even though there is no sign of a name anywhere., They held up a shirt to show me the name, and on our last day, they gave me a Cafe' Express shirt wrapped up in a gift bag!

There is a seawall around the marina with boat's names painted on it. Not even close to the scale of Horta, but it's something. Our dockmaster friend, Sergio, always loved to stop and chat with us. When he learned I was an artist he encouraged me to paint on the seawall. So I did. It was much smaller and less elaborate than in Horta, but it was a good job, and Sergio hung out the whole time and chatted and watched me paint. He seemed disappointed to stop chatting when about a hundred folks showed up for an afternoon sail on a charter boat. Sergio needed to help them get on aboard. I couldn't tell if they were more interested in my seawall painting or the task of getting on the boat, but I had a captive audience for several minutes and was asked a lot of questions.

There are several of these charter boats in Funchal. All catamarans. They do a lot of business. We saw them go in and out every day filled with people. Up on the street, the owners of these boats employed a few folks to sell rides to the passing public. They held up brochures and said "Catamaran! Catamaran!" They'd try to sell to us even after seeing us come into the marina with the dinghy and walk by every day. We'd reply "already on a boat." I thought about making up our own brochures and trying to hawk them on the street, yelling out "Tippy Monohull! Tippy Monohull!" By the second week the catamaran folks stopped trying to sell us a ride. But the restaurants all have someone standing outside their establishment saying to every single human who walks by, "Dinner? Drinks?" Even when we walked by them carrying bags of groceries, they'd say "Madam? Sir? Come in for dinner?" We held up the bags and smiled, and said "we have dinner right here." By the third week they too gave up on us.

We were ready to head along the coast to a small town called Calheta. The day Alan and Richard rented the car, we tagged along checking out a few spots. One of these spots was Calheta. We had read about this new marina in our cruising guide but there was very little information, but it seemed like a sweet spot. We decided to check it out in person. It turned out to be relatively fairly priced, and very safe inside the protective seawalls. Some swell worked its way inside but nothing like where we'd been. The folks in the marina office did offer us a deal for longer stays. We were in no hurry at this point. Our schedule had changed the moment Robert changed course for Madeira. We were actually on our route home, but it was way too early to head across the Atlantic mainly because of the weather. History has shown that weather can be rather unstable in these Atlantic waters heading east to west. Tropical storms form off Africa and move west becoming potential hurricanes. Later, starting in November and continuing through February, the winds settle into the easterly direction with the threat of hurricanes pretty much over. These are called the trade winds, because the old sailing ships carrying goods for trade rode these winds across the ocean sailing downwind, before sailors knew how to sail to weather. Our boat's insurance company actually had parameters of where and when we would be covered. They wouldn't insure us in North Africa for political reasons, but they also wouldn't insure us of we started to sail back before November, for weather reasons. Here it was July, and we had five months before a good time to head west. We decided to buy a month or more at the Calheta marina. This would give us a safe place to be if we wanted to tour the island by bus or car and avoid that heart pounding fear of on shore winds as well as get out of the rolling anchorage. (Our last day in Funchal was the rolliest ever. I swore the boat was going to roll all the way over.) Also, in Calheta, we could focus again on some boat projects. The marina folks seemed really nice, and there was a Pingo Doce grocery, our favorite, right across the street from the marina! Doesn't get much getter than this!

But it did get better!

CHAPTER 36

Good Folks, Good Sushi

We had a nice motor sail along the coast to Calheta and pulled into our slip on one hot July day. On the way, our engine started to make a weird knocking sound and at one point, we actually decided to turn around and go back to Funchal. Then the knocking sound stopped, and never came back. I guess the boat did not want to go back to the rolly anchorage.

We liked our new home for the month right away. We even heard some guys speaking English with an American accent on our dock. They were Mike and Troy from Florida who were professional captain and crew on a 45 Sport Fishing boat called Tightline. We quickly discovered that this marina was a famous spot for serious sport fishermen who were after Blue Marlin. BIG blue marlins, the kind of marlins that weigh up to 1000 pounds. All for sport. And costing millions of dollars! In the next couple of days we had met all of our sport fishing neighbors, another American named Jeff, a south African captain Alan, a Dutch crew Robin, "Frothy" a charter boat owner from Trinidad, John another charter boat owner from the UK and Tony a local. We felt right at home with them. These guys went out every single day for eight hours in search of blue marlin. Some of actual owners of the boats were there only once or twice the whole summer. Alan and Robin's boat's owner never came to Madeira. He's a South African Diamond Miner and couldn't leave home. But he kept Alan and Robin on an impressive payroll. Alan bought a house up the hill from the marina. I was able to see this cool house because Alan hired me to paint a mural inside. Another addition to international muralist status. Robin was sent to the USA to a town close to Annapolis to commission a nine million dollar custom boat being built for the next season. And to give Robin a place to stay while working on the new boat, the owner simply bought a house.

We watched these guys go out every morning, and just like clockwork, we saw them come in at 5:00. Then they'd wash down the boats and put stuff away. Jeff cranked up his music and it gave the whole dock a fun atmosphere. The locals who liked to fish for fun would occasionally ask some of these pros to join them for an evening of fishing, in exchange for some beer. The pros would say yes because they just loved to fish. One evening, we got a knock on our boat and it was Robin. He said "Would you like some fresh tuna?" Tuna? We followed him to the next dock and there on the dock were three HUGE tunas! Each one looking over 200 pounds. They were each about the size of a Toyota Prius. And Capt John from the UK was carving hunks of red sushi grade tuna meat and putting these hunks into zip lock bags and handing them out! We got two! We also had some little pieces to taste! WOW! This was better than any tuna I have ever eaten in any restaurant. Ever. This happened a few more times. Several nights while we were staying in Calheta we feasted on fresh caught tuna that I covered in sesame seeds, and then quick seared over high heat, and then dipped in soy sauce. This became our favorite way of enjoying this delicacy.

Besides sport fishing, Calheta doesn't have a whole lot of offer. There is a hotel next to the marina that sports a tiny sandy beach, the only sandy beach on the whole island. Lots of Madeirans come here for their holiday, as well as many Northern Europeans. Then there is the Pingo Doce, and a few cafes by the marina. About a quarter mile away is a police station, a bank, and a sugar mill museum, and residential homes. And that's it! Which was just fine. We proceeded to do a lot of work on the boat. I focused on the woodwork and Robert had his list of chores. We found that there was a hardware store up the hill to the left of the marina in the small town of Arco de Calheta. We needed a few supplies and decided to check it out. It was a good two – three mile hike, straight up, We found it easiest to take a bus that was headed to Funchal and get off close to the little town and walk the rest of the way. And then walk down. One day we were walking past a little hotel/guest house and I needed to use a restroom. We still had a way to go to town so I figured I'd ask in the hotel. This was a very cool hotel. The entrance was in the back, the restaurant and pool overlooked the ocean. They let me use the restroom, and as I entered I noticed many cats around the entrance.

Deed done, we continued to town. There, we found the hardware store, a few cafes, a charming mom and pop grocery store, a bank, church, hair salon, a China store, and a fruit and vegetable market. What a sweet little place! Then we decided to work our way back down to the marina by way of public paths and alleys. Some were sort of mini levada walks, and these took us through delightful areas rich with bananas, bamboo, and trees. At one point I heard the distinct sound of a kitten. The sound was coming from within a thick bamboo patch, to my right and above a small rock wall. "meeoooo, meeeoooooo." So I called back. "meeeoooooooo meeeoooooooo." (I speak kitten too.) Then I heard it louder and closer. I meeooed back and within seconds a tiny fuzzy kitten head emerged from the bamboo! He ruffled his way out, meeooooing the whole time. I picked him up, and he immediately snuggled into my neck, sitting on my shoulder. A baby kitten! He looked to be not even four weeks old. But where did he come from? We were not close to any houses. We back tracked quite a way to the nearest house, nearly a mile, and knocked. The man shook his head, the kitten was not his. We tried a few more houses with no luck. I was not about to abandon my new buddy, who I promptly named Arco de Kitty. I was his savior! Robert was worried, and I understood, that we already have two cats and one more would have been a big deal on a boat. However, we both knew we couldn't leave him. He was too young, and he was so scared, lost, and probably really hungry. Then we knew where to go. That hotel! My piss stop! I said. "Let's go back there and see if either they know where this kitten came from, or maybe they can adopt Arco." We hiked back down towards the road, with little Arco curled up next to my neck, and got to the hotel. I went in and found the owner, who smiled wide and we went outside by way of going through the kitchen where the owner grabbed a huge bag of cat food.

Outside, he filled a few bowls and dozens of cats appeared. The owner did not recognize our kitten. He did have a few older kittens who had just been weaned from their mother. But the age was clearly different. Where Arco came from was a mystery. I put my little friend down by a bowl and he looked around with big eyes at all the bigger cats. And he ate. The owner of the hotel liked Arco. I told him the kitten's name. We said our thank yous and good byes and left knowing we saved a baby cat. We returned a few days later to check on him and he not only came running up to us the second we made eye contact, but he seemed really at home with all the cats, including the cat who had weaned her older kittens and had taken Arco as her adopted baby.

When not engaging in kitten rescue, painting, varnishing, other forms of boat maintenance, we did some touring. We rented a car for one day and took several bus trips. Madeira is certainly a gorgeous island. So green and lush and vastly different from Porto Santo a mere 22 miles away! Our friendships with the fishermen grew. One day Mike from Tightline stopped by and asked if I could help him with a mural that he offered to do, for free, at a surfer bar one town away. He already told me he liked to paint and was impressed with my growing collection of little paintings that I had in the cockpit. I couldn't say no, it sounded like too much fun. He had a car. We went the next day and spent the afternoon painting away on colorful cinder block walls in a sort of indoor/outdoor bar in preparation for a big reggae concert that same night. Mike painted a sizable marlin on a dark blue wall. I painted huge fat juicy green banana leaves along one whole bright orange wall. Although we were invited to comeback and party the night away, Robert and I declined. Now I wish we had gone!

It was Mike who turned South African Capt. Alan on to the idea of a mural in his house. I spent another whole day painting an entire wall with (what else?) a huge marlin leaping out of the water. For this I got paid, and fairly well. We were invited to an end of the marlin season party which was held at Frothy's house up in the town of Arco de Calheta. We did go to this! And felt very honored to be included in the sport fisherman's event.

The end of the marlin season coincided with the end of our month. Which also meant time for another passport extension. Now we had a new issue. We were heading to the Canaries. Here's the thing, the page in our passports that was our extension said "Portugal Only." The folks back in Faro said it was possible that they may not let us off the boat in the Canaries, since it is part of Spain. They were not sure of this. They did not know much about the law. We had been e-mailing people, calling marinas in the Canaries and asking in person at the American and Spanish Embassies in Funchal since the Faro visit. We asked our friend Casey. We contacted every possible person that we could find in our cruising guide. We even became "phone friends" with the manager of the marina in Las Palmas, in the Canaries (this would become useful later.) But no one knew what to tell us. Some said we should be fine since it is all part of this 'Shengan Area." Others said we were good for Portugal only, and that we would need to get a Spanish Visa and others just had no clue. The best advice was from Brian and Dorothy, back in Funchal. "They won't even look at your passports in the Canaries" they said. But we decided to get one more extension, now that we had the routine down, and then at least we had proof that we *tried* to be legal. We found the immigration office in Funchal and paid another $180 for an extension that took us to the end of November.

CHAPTER 37

The Scariest Moment

Earlier in the summer we received an e-mail from Alan telling us he'd love to join us for the sail to the Canaries. We could have made this trip on our own but we liked Alan and enjoyed his company. We also liked the fact that he enjoyed sailing with us. Alan met us in Funchal, and once again we "vittled up" and had a final dinner out. Before we left, I called our bank, M&T, to check on things. We were really going through money fast! We tried to be extremely frugal. I didn't want to do any banking on line using public internet so I called our bank often. On this day I discovered how low our accounts had gotten, and worse, two of our credit cards were maxed out. This scared me a lot. In fact, THIS was more scary than that big storm the first night out. Hands shaking, I held back tears trying to talk intelligently in the phone. I was becoming fairly good friends with the folks at the bank and I think they enjoyed it when I called from far away places. I didn't want to sound like a downer, but I was really scared that we were going to run out of money. But Leslie at the bank told me to calm down as she looked into all of our accounts. We had money. We could pay off a hunk of the credit cards with cash, but we needed to keep cash available in a savings account. The good news was our brokerage account, one I had opened through this bank many years ago and driven by the stock market, was doing quite well. It had dropped when we arrived in the Azores, but I was too elated about crossing the ocean to care about the stock market then. Now, here we were, September 2012, and the account value had come back and then some. Enough to sell some of it to pay off one of the credit cards, the one issued by M&T, and not go below the account's principle. Leslie was licensed to buy and sell stock, so she and I finished the whole deal right there on the phone! She in her office in Annapolis, probably looking at her computer screen, and me standing in an open phone booth, across the ocean on an island looking out at all the boats in the Marina Funchal. Surreal. What an angel Leslie was. And it all worked.

Now that we had food and money, and now that I was not so scared, we sailed away from Funchal, waving goodbye to Madeira. Robert and I teared up realizing this was goodbye to Portugal! We LOVED Portugal SO much. It was like leaving a new best friend. We both are infinitely glad that we decided to spend as much time there as we did. We were getting the language down (still am to this day), we had gotten to know Portuguese food, history, traditions, daily customs, walking habits, ways of doing business, music, and so much more. We did not expect the flood of emotion that we felt seeing the island of Madeira get smaller and smaller. When we could no longer see Madeira, we wiped our tears. We focused on sailing south.

Blog: "Oh NO! We Forgot to go to the Med!"

Sep 6 2012
30:00.12 N 14:14.12 W

In one of Clive Cussler Dirk Pitt adventure novels, the two bad guys meet aboard a yacht anchored in Alexandria, Greece. As I was reading this, I realized that during this whole trip, we were never anchored in a busy ancient harbor in Greece. And this is when I realized that we forgot to go to the Med!

Actually, we didn't forget. We are right on schedule, and actually homeward bound now. We left Madeira Monday Sep 3, and headed south for the Canaries. I actually cried about leaving Portugal! I feel like I am leaving my new best friend! The adventure is no where near over, but Portugal is, at least for now.

After a month and a half in Marina Calheta, it was fun to return to Funchal. Although Calheta had its perks! It was quiet, safe, we got a lot of work done on the boat, I got a lot of painting done including a commissioned mural, an art show and one sold painting. Robert solved the mysterious 3. amp leak, installed the vented loop for the shower, changed all the filters on the engine, cleaned the bottom and a host of misc other things to get the boat ready for passage making. We met a bunch of professional deep sea fishermen and learned a lot about 1000 lb blue marlin, as well as eating the freshest tuna we had ever had. These fishermen are not just going out for an afternoon boat ride with a rig out. Some of them invest more money in the equipment than our whole boat is worth! We got to know and hang with the guys who work these boats, and it's all sport! The huge marlins get thrown back, and the huge tuna gets given away!

We also went on nightly walkabouts UP the hill either to the left or right, followed by DOWN the hill. Not much flat besides the marina, and some of the hills are so steep that down is almost as hard as up!! We will miss Calheta.

Back in Funchal, we got to enjoy the end of their annual festival celebrating the tradition of making Madeiran wine. But we had crew flying in and a great weather forecast so it was time to go.

Tomorrow we will be in the Canaries!

More MOTO Gazette to come!

CHAPTER 38

A Different World

Alan had agreed to wear a patch for seasickness. It worked, he was fine! The first night was a bit bumpy with no wind. There were some waves leftover from some previous wind. Then the breeze filled in nicely. The next day, evening, night and morning was some of the best sailing of the whole trip. PERFECT wind and wave combination and direction. *Tenacity* just flowed on down, so smooth and easy. The sound of the water whooshing by was better than music. Alan was truly enjoying it! The wind lightened but it was still a very comfortable ride. At one point, on our GPS screen, it looked as though we were going to bump right into the Western Sahara! But if course, we were not THAT close. Still, it was a cool sight.

We were greeted to a breathtaking sunrise as we approached the first island of the Canaries, Graciosa. "A MUST see, do NOT miss!" explained Brian and Dorothy. Graciosa is a small island just above and next to Lanzarote. Both quite dry and barren, but appealing and fascinating anyway.

Blog: Sailing to Graciosa

Sep 7 2012

29:13.00 13:27.00 W

My favorite point of sail is reaching, and my favorite wind speed about 12-20 knots, (for big boats) and my favorite wave conditions are waves with us. This is what we had for most of the trip here from

Funchal, it was delightful and smooth, the boat gliding along effortlessly and quiet except for the gentle slosh of water passing the hull. And then it died. The last 24 hours we motored and slowed down to a crawl so we would enter after daylight. As it was, when I got on my 6:00 AM watch, we were too close, so we actually turned around and headed out until it was light enough to see. And sure enough, we were treated to an eye popping sunrise over the northern most islands that make up the group called Lanzarote, the northern most islands in the Canaries. We are not far from North Africa, and the islands here have that kind of terrain, dusty, moonlike and tan. We motored around the bottom of Graciosa and anchored in what is a popular anchorage called Playa Francesa. By 10:00 AM, the breeze picked up out of the prevailing NE, and the people from the other anchored boats were already picking their spot on the beach, or already swimming in the crystal clear turquoise water. This anchorage is the most popular in the Canaries, but you still have to be cautious of the wind direction.

First, Robert took Alan into the beach, and later he took me in, while he dinghied around to the harbor.

I stepped out of the dinghy, into a few inches of crystal clear water and onto the soft sandy beach. From here I walked away from the water and followed what someone might call a "road," in that there was a sort of organized width of somewhat flattened, but not that flat, sand. Once considerably away from the beach, I was surrounded by sand, some lava rocks thrown in for good measure, and to my left, across about a mile of relatively flat sand land, rose a mountain of textured brown. To my right, across a few hundreds yards of sand and lava was some of the most intense blue water I have seen, and across a "channel" was more vertical brown mountain side. I kept following the "road" which at times became more flattened and easy to walk on. After about 30 minutes of walking I could see some white box like structures up ahead, clustered together, resembling a small Moroccan village or even an RV park.

As I got closer I could see vivid colorful umbrellas in the sand and sunbathers along a beach of a cove. The hot yellows and pinks against the dark turquoise, along with the multi colored swim wear of the people made this beach electric!

Then I arrived to the outskirts of Caleta del Sebo, the only town on the island of Graciosa. The roads were all sand. The cars there are all Jeeps and Land Rovers and I think one International Harvester. The buildings (mostly homes, and apartments) are bright white, flat topped, blue trimmed, no higher than three stories and clumped together around and through the few sand roads.

I arrived at the Harbor that is home to a small fishing boat anchorage, a marina, and ferry landing. Next to the ferry landing, there is a tourist souvenir shop, a few very busy cafes (when the ferry drops off its boatload of tourists) and a few hippie artists selling bracelets, tied dyed stuff, more funky jewelry and fake tattoos. Around the corner there is a bike rental place, a fruit market, two small grocery stores, a butcher, a post office, a bank (only open from 11:00 to 1:00) two more cafes hosting the island's only internet wifi, more white box buildings, three black cats and two dogs on a roof. And that is it!! The rest is the Moon!!!

The energy is happy! Laid back, but fun. The sun is hot, there is always a breeze, 20 knots from the Northeast, the norm, and so the air is actually cool. This wind is not just the prevailing wind, it's what is called the "Acceleration Zone", wind that is funneled in between these islands, Graciosa and mainland Lanzarote in this case, and increases as it gets squeezed. It's as predictable as the sun comes up.

The marina is cheap, and kept secure by Jose'. He says there is no room but I hope to charm him into suddenly finding room (rumor has it this might work) We like cheap, and even more, we really like this place!!! I have never seen a "town" like this! But then again, I have never before this been on the moon!.

Once in town, Alan parked himself at one of the busy cafes by the ferry and took in the sights and tastes. Robert and I wandered around enchanted by this place, occasionally stopping by Alan's table. We also tried to checked in with immigration, but this place was so small and laid back, they didn't even have an office.

We had heard through the cruising grape vine that the state owned marina required written permission in advance. We did try to charm the marina officials but they really did not have slips big enough. I told them I would wax our hulls up real shiny so we could slide into a smaller slip. But all we got was a chuckle and a smile. They did however offer to call another state run marina on the island of Fuerteventura, and make arrangements for us. Robert and I accepted their offer and we made a date to arrive at this other marina in less than two weeks.

We found the one little cafe that had working internet and hung there a bit catching up on social media. Back at the boat we swam and enjoyed the sunsets. Alan decided he wanted to explore more of the Canaries so he took the ferry to the island of Lanzarote, and we planned to catch up with him there later. We wanted to take advantage of this beautiful spot and stay longer. If I could turn the clock back, I would have made our arrival date to the next marina later so we could have stayed in Graciosa more days. Robert and I walked the sandy beaches, swam, explored and realized this was the first real "beach" experience we had on this trip. We did swim a bit at Calheta's tiny beach but the bottom had so many small sharp rocks it made getting in and out of the water a bit awkward. We swam that one day in Terciera but it was a cold and rainy day. We visited a beach back in Amora near the Tagus Yacht Center, but the mosquitoes were too bad. I laid on a towel on the beach next to our Oerias marina but the water was too cold to swim. We got our feet wet in Bermuda. We walked along the beach in the Algarve dressed in winter clothes. But here, anchored off of Playa Francesca, we swam in the crystal clear water, and walked all over the hot soft sandy beach. It was so nice.

After our several blissful days on Graciosa, we headed up around the northern tip and Lanzarote, and then down it's eastern coast, to the city of Arricife. There is an anchorage there that is described in the cruising guise as "protected from every direction." We found it and it was a good protected spot, but not all that pretty. Instead it was rather industrial. But we liked it anyway. We took the dinghy into the town's harbor but there was absolutely no where to land! We ended up taking the engine off, and rowing the dinghy a short distance to a small public beach, surrounded by large black lava rocks. We dragged the dinghy up onto the sand and using a long chain, locked it to a stone wall that had a drain hole. From the beach it was a mile and a half walk to the town. It was a very nice town.

Alan met us with a rental car and we toured the whole island of Lanzarote with him until evening, including another attempt at immigration check in. That office was closed. We went to a regular police station. They asked where we sailed from, we told them we sailed from Madeira to Graciosa, to here. They said, "You're fine." They didn't even ask to see our passports! All that worrying for nothing.

CHAPTER 39

Gran Tarajal

We said farewell, and shared hugs with Alan. He drove off to catch a flight back to his home. We hung for a few more days to get to know Arricife, and then headed south. We stopped for only one night right outside the entrance to Marina Rubicon in the town of Playa Blanca. Brian and Dorothy raved about this place and we even found their boat in the marina. They were not there, but we were able to charm the young lady in the office to make a call. She did and we had a nice phone reunion with our friends.

We had arrived early enough to fit in a run, swim, phone call, and a great walkabout all over Playa Blanca. We would have stayed longer but we were due to arrive at our Gran Tarajal Marina the next day. During our walkabout, we saw a boat arrive and anchor right next to us. There were a few boats already there and enough room for more. This new arrival dropped their anchor and immediately went ashore. We watched as they dinghied in, and shortly after as we continued along the promenade, we saw their boat getting very close to hitting us as it dragged through the anchorage. We were still a hike from our dinghy, but were grateful to see our anchored neighbors going out and moving this dragging boat. They finally got it to hold. Later we thanked our neighbor who helped and we shared our annoyances at sailors who do this: drop the hook and go ashore right away. Fortunately, the situation was resolved before it turned into possible damage. The folks on that boat returned and never said thanks or sorry.

We got up very early the next morning and headed to the island of Fuerteventura, to the city of Gran Tarajal, our home for the next month!

MOTO GAZETTE
Middle of the Ocean News

Eastern Atlantic Edition
September 15, 2012

Headline News

Working Class Americans Spotted On Spanish Holiday Beach

Contrary to popular belief, not all Americans have deep pockets and huge holiday spending habits.

At least two Americans, spotted recently on the island of Graciosa, a popular beach holiday island for Spaniards and Northern Europeans, are proof that there are still some Americans who pinch pennies and stick to a budget. Robert and Cindy Holden, who sailed aboard their Yacht from Annapolis Maryland to Portugal last year are living proof of this. "People here see our flag and immediately assume we are loaded" says Ms. Holden. "This boat is also our home, and our only home. Back in the U.S., when people hear we live on a boat, they think trailer trash. Here, they think big money. Funny how that works."

The Holdens have been saving for 20 years to do what they call "Robert and Cindy's Most Excellent Adventure," their primary goal having been crossing a major Ocean on their own boat. Their route has been the Atlantic Circle Route. They intend to return to Annapolis and go back to work. Their intent was to do this dream trip while they are still young enough to handle all the sailing needs and really enjoy the adventure.

But they still find themselves explaining that they are not made out of cash. "One guy, a delivery captain, when I told him we need crew because we hand steer because we don't have a decent auto pilot, he said 'Why don't you just buy one?'" says Ms. Holden. "I looked right back at him and said 'Because we can't afford it.'

Then he looked at me like I had four heads. I could have said 'We don't have a personal Gulf Stream Jet', to which he would have said "Why don't you just buy one?''

Still, these two Americans are experiencing what many would only dream of. And living on a budget in some ways has been a blessing. "We get to know all the cashiers in the local grocery stores because we don't eat out. And some of these folks have become friends!" Says Mr Holden. "Also we take buses instead of rental cars to get around and we get to see much more without the worry of driving!"

Distracted Drivers Deal with Rambling Riders

The Portuguese island of Madeira is not only known for its wine, levadas and flowers, but also its steep roads and scenic bus routes. These bus routes are carefully navigated by skilled drivers who are becoming increasingly worried about the growing population of little old ladies, who ride these buses, usually sitting in the front, and talking incessantly to the drivers. Trying not to be rude, the drivers have been putting up with all this jabbering, but lately there have too many near accidents to ignore the issue any longer. "The problem is the young people are leaving the island" says Funchal driver Manuel Silva, "These old ladies have no other way to get around. Their kids have gone to the mainland to find work, so they aren't around to drive their mothers. And these ladies are getting too old to hike up and down the steep hills." So they take to riding around on buses for not only transportation, but for entertainment, or perhaps fulfillment. Telling the driver how to live his life helps them deal with not having their kids around.

The solution? No real answer yet, but the drivers have been trying out a few options. Mr. Silva had been wearing ear bugs and listening to Fado music to block out the ladies. Henrique Fernandez, a driver in from Porto Moniz, has posted a sign "Silencioso, Por Favor," but with illiteracy still high, this has not been a successful fix.

Business News

New Arrivals from Tenacity Sea Products

The makers of EverDamp, InstaWet, and AllSalt have developed more products to make your life at home like life at sea. New this fall is RopeSkweek, A CD of the sounds of squeaking lines that is surely to lull even the most insomniac to sleep. The first in a new line of audio products.

Also not to be missed is EverGlow, a soft red light similar to the one in the compass, that installed near a bed will also ensure a good night's sleep, especially if stared at for as little as 20 minutes.

EverDamp, which already comes in 6 fantastic aromas, will have 2 more exciting aromas that surely will turn your land home into a home at sea, Unpumped Head and Dirty Shower Drain!

Police Beat

Nine sailors were arrested this past month for failing to obeying the new law that has made sailing upwind illegal and subject to fines. Marcel Wayson, of Whales, claims he was just trying to get home when Sea Police stopped him, 243 miles north of Madeira heading for mainland Europe, in a solid 20 knot breeze blowing out of the North East. Paul Lippincott, of Ireland, also claims he was just trying to get home, after being caught sailing on a beat tack from San Miguel in the Azores towards England in 15 – 20 knots of wind out of the North East. The seven other sailors were let go because they were part of a race from the Canary Islands to Madeira and therefore exempt from this law.

Blog: Western Canaries

Oct 1 2102

Of the Seven islands that make up the Canaries, the more Eastern islands are dry, closest to North Africa and less touristy than the islands to the West. The long island of Fuerteventura is the largest but least populated of the bunch. Well, Graciosa was hardly populated but that is "officially" part of Lanzarote.

Arricife, the Capital of Lanzarote, is a sizable city with a crowded busy port, crowded sun soaked beach, upscale shopping and a tall shiny hotel with a grand piano sitting in an upstairs lounge area. I know this because when we walked by this hotel on one our daily evening "walkabouts," I could practically "smell" that there was a piano nearby. We waltzed right in, I stomped right up the stairs, saw it, sat right done and played for an hour. This is what happens when you have "Piano Withdrawal." Apparently I played OK. NO one asked us to leave and people clapped.

The town of Playa Blanca is on the southern tip of Lanzarote. It is a tourists saturated beach city with very little Spanish feel. More like Disney Land. But still, a happy place, and a very pretty beach and an old harbor.

Fuerteventura is practically spitting distance from Play Blanca. And sailing down the Eastern coast of this island is like sailing along a lot of sloping brown and gray rock. No development, except a sprinkling here and there, and no green. The city of Gran Tarajal is towards the bottom and for Feurteventura, a fairly big town, although there are one or two bigger This town has a great beach and a little "bay," where boats can anchor provided the wind is not from the south.

Along the beach is a busy waterfront promenade where all the town's nicer cafes and restaurants are. To the south of town is the boatyard and marina. In town, there are a few small cafes, some lively bars, a well manicured and active park, two gas stations, three sporting good stores, a few grocery stores, (two big,) a few banks, some clothing stores, one sort of "Department Store," a vet, about five bread stores, a book store, a "paper/stationary" store, a liquor store, a kids' toy store, one chandlery, two hardware stores, one China store, and excellent art supply and paint store, two cell phone stores and about fifty hair salons. All local, not a tourist shop in sight!!! Not even a postcard stand!!! And good thing they have hair salons!

In the recent past, Gran Tarajal was a popular hiding place for outlaws, drug runners and misfits avoiding civilization and authority. Even though this is not the case now, the marina still has some pretty serious security guards wandering around. We tied up in an available slip and went to the office to sign in. A very tall, gun wielding non smiling guy approached us. He was Christopher. Huge, solid muscle, bald, and all business. He had us move to a different (and better) slip and we finished our formalities at the marina office. I saw right through this guy. Just something about him, or maybe pure instinct, but I was betting he was as sweet as a kitten inside this rough exterior. Sure enough, later, we saw him in town with his wife and little daughter and he cooed over his daughter, smiled and giggled. Any toughness that was there before was completely absent. He was as nice and sweet as I figured!

We settled into our new home and got into a routine. We quickly, of course, fell in love with Gran Tarajal.

Blog: Six Reasons Why We Love Gran Tarajal

Oct 6 2012

28:12.05N 14:01.05 W

Every where we go, we find reasons to fall in love with the place. There has yet been a place we haven't liked. Even places that were not rated all that great by other cruisers, we found beauty in the people, the surrounding neighborhoods and of course, cats.

Gran Tarajal has gotten mixed reviews. The cruising guide calls it "unspoilt," true, and the various web sites call it "more like the Canaries before tourism really set in," also true. But we've met more than one other cruiser who just find it "boring," or said "they've seen enough," or "not a nice town." NOT TRUE!!!!!!!!!!!!

They just didn't get the same experience that we have had so far!! We love this town. And here are just 6 reasons (so far) why we so much like it, in no particular order!

#1 Song Birds. There are song birds here, but so few trees. So the song birds are concentrated in the trees that are in the town's center square and park. And they are LOUD birds! Louder than the 17 year Cicadas. SO MANY birds in a tight area make for one of the oddest sounds I have heard. It's musical, a bit of a shrill, and a wonderful sound as we walk through the busy town's square.

#2 The Busy Town Square. We noticed this back in Ayamonte, that in Spain, the city squares get busy and full of families of many overlapping generations out just enjoying being outside. Here in Gran Tarajal, this square is along the waterfront, and beach. There is a playground on the actual beach. There are several benches in the square, and there are cafes all along the waterfront. By early evening the place is hopping with little kids, older kids, teenagers, young adults, middle age, aging adults, old and really old people, all interacting, talking, playing, laughing, eating, drinking, sitting, watching and strolling. And these are locals! It is a very positive energy!

#3. Old Farts Sitting on Their Benches. Closer to the boatyard and marina, there are a bunch of old guys who sit and hang out, probably discussing the world, often through out the day. They start out beside a little fish restaurant that is right next to the boatyard. And then later when that spot gets too hot from the sun, they move up to two benches on a hill. I got the guts one day to stop and photograph them. They, of course saw me, so I waved, They waved back! Now they smile and wave every time we walk by!! We smile and wave back. It is my intention and duty to go up to the hill bench before we leave, and join them, so Robert can take our photo, with me sitting with the old farts, smiling and waving!

#4 The Casa de Cultural. There is this school/cultural center that offers free internet Wi-Fi connection. We have been going there pretty much every day. So have other cruisers. There is a "cubicle" in the middle of the lobby that has seats, and plugs for battery chargers. We met a local lady who is teaching an English class there in the evenings. She asked us one night to be her "special guests" and talk to her class in English. She liked that we speak in American English. So we did! We all went around and introduced ourselves! Now, we often see one of the students, Edgar, around town and he calls out to us, "Robert! Cindy!" and comes over and says hello, talks in English. He even invited us out for a drink!! This is special in my book!!! Also the cleaning lady in the school is also one of the cleaning ladies at the marina. She loves to show me the books that are available for us to take and read. But they are in German and won't do me any good. But she is such a sweetheart!

#5 The Other Cleaning Lady at the Marina. I haven't gotten her name yet, or the other one. But this one lady is always out around the marina cleaning up, keeping blown gravel off the walking paths and she does general maintenance. Our favorite part is she also polishes the metal lamp posts. They look like shiny aluminum. But she is about 5' 4", and her polishing brush is about as long as a broom handle. So the 20 ft. high lamp posts are only shiny as far up as she can reach! She is out there every day! And she always always stops to say hello to us. She is great.

#6 The Land of Trees!! We have counted each and every tree in the actual city of Gran Tarajal and have come up with 729 trees!!! Where else can one actually count all the trees in town? The land is so incredibly barren, they really had to make an effort to have even this many trees here. Did we ever get some looks as we walked around pointing, tapping and counting. So now we know there are 729 trees. Although we didn't count the baby trees. If we visit again in a dozen years or so, there will be quite a bit more.

This place is so dry they get about four hours of rain a year. And we got it while we were there! One day when we were at the Casa de Cultural reading e-mail or watching kitten videos on facebook, it started to rain and the people ran to the door and looked outside. It was like people in Florida seeing snow! Alan had learned from locals during his explorations that they cultivate the morning dew to get water for vegetation. They also have a sea water desalination plant. But rain is rare!

It had turned out to be a good thing we arrived when we did because the marina filled up. At one point there was a hurricane predicted to blow through, although the immediate forecast was not too bad. Every single slip was taken. The night the hurricane was supposed to blow through we saw no more than 30 knots of wind. Still, we had a good slip, and the marina became a busy place. We were invited aboard one boat for beers during this hurricane buzz. Ordinarily I would say it was a great visit. But it was odd. The hosts of this happy hour were a couple from Scotland. The guy said rather insulting things about his wife and she put up with it. Then the guy pulled out his guitar, passed around printed lyrics and started to sing. He sang a song he wrote about sailing along through life without a care in the world. The moment was very awkward. Robert and I really liked the other couples that were there, but I was not liking this guy and his wife bashing and song singing pushing. Cruising can have its blissful moment, sure, but there are things that need to be cared about. We know it was just a song, but the guy was not someone we wanted to get to know. His insults toward his wife were bad enough to write him off. The situation made me think about the stereotypes of cruisers. There are those who do sail off into the sunset and leave all worries behind. I guess we don't fit in that group. We left with worries, but worthwhile ones. We left knowing we had friends facing major health issues. We wanted to make sure our bills would be paid. We still wanted to be upstanding citizens when we returned as well as legal travelers abroad. We still considered ourselves "professionals" even while cruising. We prayed and thought about our troubled friends and discovered later that they ended up just fine. We left the happy hour after a couple of beers. This guy was the only person we met that we didn't like.

We were in Gran Tarajal during Robert's birthday, and decided to treat him, and us, to a camel safari, that we had read about in the cruising guide. We learned from the locals that there was a large zoo called Oasis Park a bus ride away. It offered camel safaris and we were told it was an outstanding park. We got up early on a dazzling clear morning and rode the bus to Oasis Park. We were advised to do the safari early before the day's heat sets in. We were also advised to get the front camel, since they might fart. We chose our camel, named "Louis" and enjoyed our hour long safari sitting in leather seats strapped over the camel's hump and went up a good long sandy hill with incredible views. We rode back down, experiencing the rocky wobbly ride as the camels' long spindly legs navigated the rocky terrain. We were the only ones in the whole camel train that didn't have to hold on since we were already used to the motion of the ocean! The other riders were gripping the seats' rails with white knuckles and had their knees and legs glued together on the little steps under the seats. We sat back, put our feet up on the camel's hump, and waved at the guy with the video camera, changing our position each time we saw him to "shake things up" for the video. The video guy earlier walked along the train of seated camels with awaiting riders in their seats, selling orders for this video. We bought one, and watching it later, we did provide some entertaining variety among the stiff and scared riders behind us. We thoroughly enjoyed our camel Louis, the other camels, (no one farted) the ride and the later the whole wonderful day at Oasis Park! We stayed until the very very end. We met all the animals. Robert bonded with a giraffe who ate out of his hand. There was a smartly built porch at the giraffes' head's height. The park provided stalks of grass and bamboo to hold out for these giraffes. These gentle creatures strolled to the porch and greeted the humans holding grass. One even nuzzled Robert's neck. Oasis Park is enormous. I bonded with the camels, hugging several, and stroking their enormous fuzzy heads. Even though we stayed until the last minute, we both agreed we could have easily stayed longer.

With the park closed for the day, we waited for our return bus. But no bus came. It was getting later and later, but that was not the issue. The issue was that the camels that had been in the safari area were now put away for the night. The flies that had been hanging around the camels were now hanging around Robert and me. And they were biting bad. We were thinking that we had gotten the time wrong for the bus return trip. It could be another hour, at least, if at all, before a bus came. This was not good. The flies got worse, so we put out our thumbs and hitch hiked. Hitch hiking any where is a risk, and there we were in a foreign country. But sure enough, a couple of young adventurers from Wales stopped and drove us all the way back to Gran Tarajal. This day of camels, giraffes, flies and hitch hiking was one of our favorite days of the trip.

While in Gran Tarajal, we got lots of boat work done. *Tenacity* was getting into better shape than before we left Annapolis. I had gotten many coats of varnish on all the wood and it was really getting shiny! I polished all the stainless steel. I sanded and painted the trim on the hatches as well as the compass binnacle and any and all nicks around the whole boat. Robert stripped the floor inside the head, made sure the bulkhead was not wet, prepped the floor and laid a new layer of fiberglass. This was a big job. I cleaned and varnished all the wood inside the head and painted some of the sliding doors a bright teal that made it look like a 1960's era Chris Craft.

I decided it was time to paint eyes on the bow. I had wanted to do this for years. Decades in fact! I had painted eyes on my old wooden *Tenacity* at the advice of a friend in Beaufort. He asked me, "Would you ride a blind horse? How will you see in the fog?" Now here, in Gran Tarajal, Robert was convinced we should have eyes. I painted them and felt better about everything as a result.

One day a boat from Australia pulled in. It had a family of four, John, from Australia, his German wife Karen and their two kids, Lizzy and Finn. We helped them tie up and John and Robert got to talking right away about where to get propane tanks filled. We were already researching this. In Spain, it not as easy to get propane as in Portugal. John and Robert made a plan to go together to a gas station and try there. When John stopped by our boat to get Robert, I was working on a little painting. He was impressed, and hired me to paint a portrait of his boat. A commission! We agreed on a price and I got right on it.

Robert came back with not so good news. Getting our tanks filled in Spain might be an issue, bigger than we thought, due to our American tank fittings. Apparently, some one had an explosion while filling an American style tank. Therefore they (Spain) simply made it illegal to fill American tanks. We would need to really ask around the cruising grape vine. John scored because even though his boat was an American boat, he had English tanks. We probably had enough propane for the crossing, but it would sure be nice to top them off.

Back when we were in Calheta, I had received a notice from my buddies at the bank that my tenant's rent checks had stopped coming in. I had kept my studio and rented it out to two different young guys. One rented my studio, and the other rented the space that is next to the studio. The spaces share a wall. My lease includes both spaces and I was paying for the rent the whole time. The two guys were paying me by sending the checks right to the bank. I made a phone call and the bad news was confirmed. The tenant renting the front space walked out. This was not good. I didn't want to lose the space. It was and still is one of the best spots in Annapolis. I made a few calls to put the word out that there was office space for rent. Then I went to social media for help. I put out a plea on Facebook and very quickly received a response from an old friend, Karen, who said she was interested. And she took it! This started an e-mail dialog between Karen and me. In Gran Tarajal, this dialog continued. Karen cleaned up the space, painted the walls and made it beautiful. In one e-mail, she said she had a fantasy about helping us sail our boat back across the ocean. This was amazing timing because we needed to get serious about finding crew. We already knew Karen and knew she had the perfect adventurous spirit and enough sailing experience to be great crew. We continued this new conversation and she sealed the deal with airline tickets! This was good news!

Now we had one crew. We needed to think about heading to Las Palmas. Our choice for a departure point. After a month and two weeks we wrapped up our goodbyes in Gran Tarajal and headed to the island of Gran Canaria. We knew we would miss Gran Tarajal. It was a treat. Again, we loved our stay, but it was time to move on.

On the way to Gran Canaria we anchored one night off the town of Morre Jabble, a bit of a disconcerting anchorage since the entire Atlantic Ocean was right there behind us. But it has a reputation as "safe." What's even more weird is right around the bend from our anchorage is where some international windsurfing events take place. The bend at the bottom of Fuerteventura is just enough to make the difference between epic windsurf wind to compete in and a gentle breeze to sleep by. We had taken a bus a week earlier to see Morre Jabble. We were warned by other cruisers that it was dirty and not to go there. But, we found it charming, clean, and alluring. Next to the town is a long popular beach full of sun-seeking tourists. However, it didn't offer a safe place for a boat to stay except in a small marina that was full. After a quiet night anchored in the ocean, we got up with the sun and headed west. The 60 mile sail was uneventful. We arrived in Las Palmas in plenty of time to check in, get into a "slip" and go for a five mile run before dark.

CHAPTER 39

Las Palmas: Last Stop In Europe

At the Las Palmas marina, they have you come into the floating dock either bow in or stern in. There are no finger piers so the guy at the helm (me) really has to be careful not to side swipe the neighboring boats. The dock attendant hands an end of a line to whoever takes it. This line is attached to a mooring further away than an average boat's length from the dock. Whoever takes the line from the attendant then walks it to the stern (if you're bow in) and ties it off. By this time, the line is completely slimy, wet, muddy and gross.

We needed to have fenders out before we pulled in, and our new neighbors were there and ready to put out their fenders. Once in, the next challenge is getting on or off the boat. We saw a lot of boats stern in with gang planks. We preferred to be bow in, it's just more private that way. We put out a little portable step that we hung off the port bow so we could step down and up with some sort of ease. It got easier as we did it more. Over all, this is not our favorite docking situation. But we got used to it. It does allow the marina to squeeze a lot more boats. The price was great! 10 Euros a night, that included water, electricity, a locked gate at the end of the dock, and a locked gate at night at the street entrance although there was no word of crime. They even fumigated the docks for roaches, an added plus. Also, that 10 Euros got us showers, if we wanted, in more than one building.

We had heard and read that the marina fills up starting in late September for the annual ARC regatta. ARC stands for Atlantic Rally for Cruisers. In fact, even slip holders that pay annually leave from September through November. We met some of these folks in Gran Tarajal. They said, "Don't even try to get in that marina!" Well,

Robert had already gotten to "know" Frenando on the phone when he was calling about the passport issue. Fernando told him to call first to see if there was room. He had said if there was room we could come on in! The day we arrived they had room. There is an anchorage, with a somewhat good reputation. But it was really crowded and we decided to stay at the marina until they told us to leave, which we were warned would happen when all the ARC boats arrived. We were also told to check in at the office daily, to see if we could stay another day. This turned out to be a social event. We would wait in line with a bunch of other cruisers swapping sea stories. Including John and Karen, the couple we met in Gran Tarajal and whose boat portrait that I was painting was almost complete. John and Karen were part of the ARC regatta. They arrived in Las Palmas a few days before us.

We leaned that there had been really nasty weather back near Gibraltar, all related to that hurricane we never got, and it was delaying most of the ARC boats. This meant there really was some room in the marina. But it sort of depended on who you ask. It was rumored that it also kind of depended on if they "like" you in the office. The first day that we waited in line, we saw Fernando through the window. Good! We liked Fernando and he liked us. And sure enough, when it was our turn, he chatted with us like we were old buddies. Although his English was perfect, we still let him know that we wanted to try to speak some Spanish. Our Spanish was improving on Graciosa. Not only is it really fun to learn new languages, but the locals really appreciate it. Fernando gave us two more nights, but did say to check in the third day. If there was room he'd let us stay. 10 Euros a night was not a whole lot more than running the engine every day to charge the batteries. Also, they charged two Euros a day for the anchorage (grrrrrmumble) but at least for two Euros, you got to use the dinghy dock, and the showers. So there was some value there, when we would need it.

This business went on for over two weeks. If we didn't get Fernando we'd be as nice as possible to who ever was in the office and try to speak Spanish. One day we got the marina owner's daughter, who we learned did not like cruisers who did not speak Spanish. She would often send them away with a lame apology. Robert and I saw a cat photo on her desk and started to tell her about our cats, who now had Spanish Passports. This broke the ice, got her to smile and she let us stay! The day did come when all the ARC boats had arrived and we headed out to the anchorage.

CHAPTER 40

Work!

We noticed right away in Las Palmas a different kind of buzz than anywhere else. Almost all the sailors were getting ready for a big trip. Many were like us, getting ready to sail across the ocean. A lot of sailors were part of the ARC. Many of the ARC participants are experienced, but many more not. Which is what makes a group ocean crossing so appealing. However it is very expensive to be a part of this adventure. It costs $3000 just to sign up. Then there is all the other stuff. There was money here, and these guys were spending it. As opposed to most of Portugal, where the people didn't have a lot of money to spend on things like yachting. Here yachting was the big deal.

I made a banner that read, on two sides; "BOAT LETTERING, SAIL REPAIR, and "Small Paintings For Sale." I also made fliers with photos of paintings, including the commission that I had finally finished for John and Karen ($300!) I hung these up around the marina. Almost immediately Robert got a sail repair job! And I got a job to repair a damaged oil painting, and later a lettering job. Then at the anchorage, Robert got some canvas work. He made enough money to cover all of our marina dock fees! I had offered to give art lessons to John and Karen's kids. They were so enchanted with my painting I just wanted to do it. Karen set me up in their boat, a Swan 51 named Senta, and we, the kids, Karen and I, all had SO much fun. It became a regular thing. Karen would call the other parents involved in the ARC regatta to let them know she was hosting Art Afternoons. I cherished Art Afternoons! This was all too good to even think about leaving this place. We stayed there until our crew arrived.

CHAPTER 41

Fully Crewed!

We already knew Karen from Annapolis was coming. One day, we received an e-mail from John Prehn saying he wanted to join us for the sail back! Wow! This was tremendous news! They even had the same schedules, and were flying to meet us on Dec 15th. We had a plan. We also had a lot of things to do in Las Palmas. Including of course, daily walkabouts, two car rental days, and more boat work. We did find a local who filled our propane tanks (don't tell anyone, he was doing it on the sneak). We enjoyed getting to know more fellow cruisers.

In spite of the fact we were set for crew, we couldn't help notice all the young travelers that hung around the marina looking for a boat to get on as crew. These kids would eyeball us from across the marina and walk right up and ask if we needed crew. Robert and I felt like magnets to these kids. We got to know a few and helped them find a boat. We liked them. But we didn't have room for more. Besides lack of room though, we did not want to take on one of these kids. Most of them had not a lick of sailing experience. They were just looking for adventure!

Blog: Dreamers and Dreadlocks

Nov 12, 2012
28:07.06N 15:25.05W

When one chooses to live their life in a non conformist style, they intentionally dress different than the "norm," they wear their hair different, choose unusual ways to earn money and see themselves as "outside" society. That is until they all arrive at the same place at the same time like bikers at a Harley Davidson convention.

Here in Las Palmas, the capital city of the Canary Islands, during the months of October and November, a different kind of convention takes place. This is the official starting location for the annual ARC event, the Atlantic Rally for Cruisers. This is an excellent place for cruisers to begin the trip across the Atlantic Ocean during the trade winds.

Over the years, word as gotten out that if you are a young traveler who dreams of adventure, this is the place to be to look for a berth on a boat sailing to the Caribbean, South America, or as some of the fliers say: "Where ever the wind takes us." These young folks walk around and approach people they suspect are boat types and ask, super politely, if they are looking for crew. They also post notices around the marina advertising their dreams, and maybe even a few skills. One guy brags that he is an experienced clown. Another can play guitar. Another can juggle. These young dreamers look pretty much alike. They must have gotten the "How To Look Like Traveling Dreamer" handbook before they arrived in Las Palmas. For example, most of them have dreadlocks, and wear little beaded things in their hair. They all seem to wear the usual wrist, neck and ankle woven decorations. Many carry guitars. Most wear cargo type shorts and loose gingham shirts, or surf board shorts and worn out earthy colored T shirts. A lot of them have huge backpacks. Many claim to like cooking. And then there is that clown.

We asked one sweet American girl if she knew how to sail, and she responded with "I've never been on a boat!!" ???? Does she know it's an OCEAN she wants to sail across?? Some do have experience, and a few have a lot of experience. These ones look more like sailors, well at least they don't have the "required" dreadlocks, and they don't seem to be carrying guitars.

The fliers are works of art in themselves. Some have cute little kokapelli cartoons on them and say things like "Take me, I am young and like to cook and clean up after you! I've worked as a grape cutter in France and as a tattoo artist in the Croatia. I will entertain you with my guitar! I have no sailing experience but I am eager to learn." Or "I know how to juggle!"

Do they know if they get seasick? And does anyone need a grape cutter or a tattoo artist to sail across the ocean?

But one thing that is a bit baffling to us, is so many of them approach Robert and me. They weren't approaching some og our neighbors, who clearly have bigger boats. But they glom right to me and Robert. Then I realized that I also wear woven things on my wrists and ankles and I wear board shorts, and have long hair that I try but can't seem to keep brushed in this windy weather. (Maybe dreadlocks are the answer.) So maybe they approach us because we *"look" like them? uh oh. This may be so, but I am not going to carry a piano around!*

Tenacity returned to the marina once the ARC boats left. We got busy getting ready for John and Karen and the trip. This was going to be our second Atlantic crossing. We were pretty relaxed about it this time. The boat was pretty much ready. Just some minor things to do. We installed an exhaust fan in the forward cabin to draw in fresh air from the main salon, and we installed two new electric fans that use a whole lot less power than our old ones. At sea, the forward cabin can get stuffy, and if we open the hatch, waves come right on in. So now with the exhaust fan and two new air fans, we were hoping to keep the stuffy factor to a minimum. I applied as much varnish as I could on all the wood. We laundered all the bedding and stowed stuff away. On Dec 15, our crew arrived! We were about to officially leave Europe.

Thinking back to the day of our arrival in the Azores, I remembered what Duncan Spencer had said in Horta. "Europe doesn't get any better than right here." Well, I still can't say if I agree. Horta was beyond special in so many ways. But every place we went to was special. We saw much of Europe in a way that most travelers would not. We got to become familiar with the local people. Made many friends. We hiked through back alleys, visited off beat cafes and met many shop owners. We got to know the local music, the trendy Euro fashions, even bought funky shoes. We saw ancient castles, exquisite beaches, alluring villages and bustling cities. We befriended cats and camels and even a giraffe. We loved it all. I think I would have to not agree with Duncan. Horta was probably a favorite place, especially magical being the first stop after almost 3000 miles. But we loved it all. As we got closer to leaving, I realized that I was really, really sad to be leaving Europe. But it was time. It was time to go.

CHAPTER 41

Leaving Las Palmas and An Unplanned Detour

The boat was ready, we were ready, and our crew was ready and excited to cross the ocean.

As we did with Richard and Alan, we let John and Karen get adjusted to the new time zone, and to see some of Las Palmas. We had fallen in love with Las Palmas (oh, big surprise!) We were excited to show them "our" new city. After a few days of sight seeing and grocery shopping, the time had come to shove off. We stowed all the food, washed the decks, filled the water tanks, and proceeded to the fuel dock to fill up, settle up and head out. We untied the lines and motored out of the marina. What a difference from leaving the Chesapeake Bay. This seemed so easy!

The weather forecast was for a very light breeze to build. We had enough breeze to sail and it was just perfect for Karen's first day and night offshore. On day three, the engine would not start. By this time there was plenty of wind for sailing. However we still wanted to top off the batteries with that one hour of engine running. Robert and I both tried to bleed it with no success. He traced every fuel line, and by the end the fourth day, we both concluded that fuel was getting into the injector pump, but not getting out. We kept sailing along, but needed to be very frugal with power. The wind was directly behind us, meaning the wind generator only put out a little juice. We sailed a bit easterly to get more wind across the deck and into the generator. We needed to make a decision. We could turn back, which would be back tracking, and when the wind picked up, it would be from the north and we'd be beating, but this was an option. We could just sail across the ocean, but if there was water inside the engine, which was the likely, it could do a whole lot more damage than just the pump. Water could maybe ruin the whole engine, which we really did not want to do. Removing the injector pump was not really an option. It's a highly complicated thing. It needs to be fine tuned and calibrated before putting it together and this usually requires a machine shop. Another option was to detour to Cape Verde, and get the thing fixed.

With our Sat phone, we e-mailed the contact person in Cape Verde, Kai Brossman, a German Engineer who now owns a marina in the capital city of Mindelo on the island of St. Vincent. We got his e-mail from our cruising guide. Kai said he could fix us up and to come on down. He'd even arrange to have a marina skiff come out when we got to the harbor and escort us into a slip. Karen and I began speculating on what this Mr. Kai Brossman looked like. He had, in the cruising guide, quite a reputation. We looked forward to our detour and meeting this guy.

Since we were already heading generally south anyway, to get into the trade winds, we really didn't do much in the way of adjusting course. The ancient advice for seafarers leaving the Canaries is to "sail South till the butter melts, then turn West". The wind picked up as predicted and by Christmas day, we were surfing down 12 ft waves in 20 – 30 knots of wind! Too rough for a big turkey dinner but we had a blast belting out Christmas Carols while surfing down the Atlantic.

On the morning of the 27th, we saw land and sailed towards the harbor of Mindelo. We were warned of the "Venturi Effect" when wind gets squeezed between islands. This was called the "Acceleration Zone" in the Canaries, and it didn't pose that much of a problem, mainly because we were going downwind. What did become a problem was the downdrafts from the mountain sides as we entered the harbor. The wind in the harbor went from 10 – 15 knots, gusting to 35 knots in a blink of an eye. It was a very crowded harbor with yachts, fishing boats, derelict boats, ferries, ships, some moving some not, little work boats, big boats, barges, half sunk barges, all different colors and degrees of dilapidation and we were sailing right through this mess, tacking back and forth, avoiding other boats by inches, all the while trying to talk to Tuga, the dockmaster at the fuel dock, on the radio. We were too early for Kai and his skiff, but Tuga knew who we were, and that we had no engine. We tacked back and forth and saw Tuga's guys coming out in an inflatable. He said what I thought was "Take your sail down." What he did say was something to the effect of "come sail on down" but between the radio crackle and his OK English, I heard "Take the sail down." We rolled in the jib. Bad idea. Just as the jib was rolled up, we saw that the guys in the inflatable were now rowing with their engine pulled up. This meant we were free drifting through the harbor at about five knots at the mercy of the wind and current. We were too busy getting ready to fend off boats at this point to roll the jib back out. Several people on anchored boats were watching and jumped in their dinghies to help. With the help of another cruiser in his dinghy, we drifted right towards an open spot and dropped the anchor and stopped. After a deep breath, and bowing to some cheering from the anchorage at our spectacular sailing, we hung out and waited for the marina to open. By 10:00 AM we were safe in a slip and the guys were looking at our engine.

Cape Verde is a poor West African island nation. When Kai Brossman decided to start a marina with repair facilities in Mindelo, he was considered almost a savior! He took in young kids and trained them to do marine related work like engine repair, welding, electrical work, painting, and more. They not only worked really hard, but were loving it. They got on our injector pump job right away even though it was the holiday season.

It didn't take long to discover we had taken on horrible fuel in Las Palmas. Dirty gunky fuel that was almost more water than fuel. In Europe, the diesel is clear, so you can't tell by looking at it that water is in there. We were the fifth boat that season who had arrived in Mindelo from Las Palmas with bad fuel. We also heard from John and Karen on Yacht Senta that a third of the ARC boats bought bad fuel in Las Palmas and many had injector pump problems. The fact that we weren't alone wouldn't fix the problem, but it made us feel better. Kai and his guys had to take the pump off and replace a broken shaft inside. This would only take a few days and they didn't have to order any parts. Good news. We also needed to pump out all that fuel and replace it. Ugh. It had to be done however if we wanted a working engine.

Meanwhile, Karen and John and I hit the town in search of a laundromat and groceries and found a marvelous city with old cobblestone alleys, colorful buildings, a waterfront main street, a large festive market selling everything from beaded jewelry to soccer shoes and ladies in the streets selling fruits and veggies. We did find decent grocery stores and a park where we could get free wifi. We were liking this place! We cooked our big Christmas turkey dinner with all the trimmings and got to know Mindelo while our pump was being fixed. It has all the characteristics of what the words "Third World Country" conjures up. At one point in history, Portugal ruled these islands and the architecture is still European, blended with plain concrete buildings, all boasting crumbly colorful painted surfaces oozing with character. Occasional dogs roamed a street. Although the people are poor, the atmosphere is friendly. The markets are lively. The weather was hot but nice. I could see how Mr. Brossman was attracted. I felt safe running in the mornings and discovered terrific routes through old neighborhoods and along the far end of the harbor. Another place to love!

CHAPTER 42

Last Tango in Mindelo

On New Years Eve, John and I were buying groceries from the ladies in the street. When I reached for my wallet in my backpack to pay for a fish, my wallet was gone. I couldn't believe it! I went ballistic! John kept trying to calm me down, telling me it's how we react to situations that matters. As I look back on this day, I realize now why I was so horribly upset, (crying and shaking, the works). During our whole cruise, we were able to adjust to every situation and "fix it" ourselves, with a tool, or a bolt, or a hose clamp. The broken steering arm during the tornado didn't set me off. But this wallet theft was an offense. Someone had unzipped my pack and took something that belonged to me. I couldn't just reach for the tool box and fix it.

One lady who owns a cafe felt bad for me and took me inside and sat me down while she called the police. The police came, and on our way to the station, a guy stopped the car and said he saw who took the wallet. It was the "town thief." He had just gotten out of jail! The police were very nice and even said there was a good chance they'd find the wallet. They knew the guy who stole it. (His name is Patrick Ramano, by the way.) I explained that we were on our boat *Tenacity* at the only marina in Mindelo. We finished up with all the formalities and went back to the boat.

Robert was happy because the pump was fixed, back on and the engine was running! But I had to give him the bad news about the wallet. After a while, I had calmed down and accepted what had happened. Still, I was really upset. Robert was upset but he was more happy about the engine. We could deal with the wallet.

After dinner that night, John and Karen encouraged Robert and I to have a little "together time." It was News years Eve, and they said we should go walking around town.

On our way up the dock, we were stopped by the marina security guard who gave us a handwritten note, that said "Tenacity, wallet found." They found it! We excitedly went to the police station.

When we arrived at the station, there were six angry young men in front of us. They were having a very excitable argument over something and it was going to become a fist fight. They actually went TO the police to mitigate the argument. One of the guys was escorted into a small office, the very one I was in giving my report to the police, and the officer closed the door and lowered the window blinds. This left Robert, me, five angry young men and a woman guard in the waiting room. The young guys were still arguing, firing away in rapid Creole/Portuguese, poking each other in the shoulders, and occasionally spitting. The waiting room was spartan. It had old wobbly chairs with worn and torn vinyl seats, a green and white tile floor, a cracked window over looking the street, and a TV mounted on a stand up high on the wall. The TV was playing the Portuguese version of "Dancing With The Stars".

On this evening, in the police station, we noticed the dancers on the TV were wearing what looked like Bavarian clothing and dancing to a tango beat. This is just wrong. We were commenting on this as the five angry young men continued their yelling and poking and spitting. One of them noticed us talking about the TV show and looked up at the TV and back to us with a quizzical look on his face. We kept critiquing the dancing, as the yelling got a bit quieter and the young men started to pay more attention to us, than their argument, whatever it was about. After a while, I noticed silence. The rapid speaking had subsided, and replaced with completely confused staring at us weird white people watching Dancing With The Stars. I said, in English, to the guys, "we do this" while pointing to the TV, "Only we do it on ice in skates" (as if they understood.) The woman guard spoke English and I spotted her holding back a smile. I tried a few Portuguese words, but found better success with pointing and hand language, trying to communicate "We know this music is supposed to be the tango, and their costumes are all wrong. We know the Tango." The guys kept staring at us with wide eyes and in disbelief, the guard kept suppressing a smile. I said, in English "Would you like us to demonstrate?" No response from the guys, the woman guard was now smiling. Then, Robert and I got up, and danced the Tango across the old tiled floor of a third world police station while being watched in awe by five angry young men and silently applauded by one woman guard.

At the end of the dance, we sat and smiled. And so did the guys! The woman guard was now smiling ear to ear. It was moment I will never ever forget. I wonder if the guys even remembered what they were fighting about. But the officer in the closed room was not finished. It was almost midnight. We said we would come back in the morning to check on our wallet. As we left, five pairs of wide eyes followed us out of the room.

We headed to the main street in town where there was a stage set up with live music playing hauntingly beautiful Cape Verdian tunes, and since we were already warmed up, we danced in the street with the crowds of partiers. People started pulling out their phones and filming us, (even in poor third world cities everyone has a smart phone.) They clapped for us! We got back to the boat just in time to join Karen and John on deck to watch a dazzling display of fireworks as the clock hit midnight.

CHAPTER 43

Serenading Cop

The next morning, I returned early to the police station. People were still partying in the street. They had been there all night long. When I arrived to the station, there was a German couple ahead of me. They were very, very upset. It turned out they had everything stolen, their passports, wallets, computer, camera, etc, probably by my buddy Patrick Ramano, now on a stealing binge. I again waited in the little waiting room, the TV now off. A young cop was there who spoke a little English. He asked me about how I liked my stay in Mindelo. I told him with the exception of Mr. Ramano, I loved it. We went outside and watched the parade of tired sleepless people march by with a live band playing the same song we had been hearing all night and the same one we danced to in the street. It was the Cape Verdian New Year's Song, their version of our Auld Lang Syne song. The cop asked me if I knew the song, I only told him I had heard it all night and that I thought it was very beautiful. He then proceeded to sing it to me in both Portuguese and English. There I was, standing on the steps of West African Island Nation's capital city police station being serenaded by a young police officer. It was surreal.

After the grieving German couple left, I went in and said I was there to pick up my wallet. The officer started to actually look under old pizza boxes and open and close drawers, all the while saying he didn't know of my wallet. I could tell this wasn't going to be good. The police had been understaffed on their busiest day of the year. Our wallet was way far down the chain of concern. Someone had found it, or we wouldn't have gotten that note. But then it got put somewhere and that was the end of it.

CHAPTER 43

Time to Cross The Ocean, Again

We gave up on the wallet. On our last day, we settled up with the marina, filled up our empty fuel tanks, signed out of immigration, picked up a few more groceries, and headed out once again to cross the ocean, sans wallet.

We did experience some fairly serious venturi effect as we sailed away from Sao Vincent island with Sao Antao to our right. It was blowing a solid 35 on our tail. We were in the "Acceleration Zone" and as soon as we sailed past Sao Antao we arrived in what the cruising guide calls the "Windshadow." This is a windless "shadow" that according to the guide can extend 20 miles past the island's tip. We surfed with speed and exhilaration right on through the Acceleration Zone and came to a screeching halt as we entered the windshadow. Reading about and experiencing these wind effects made me compare these wind terms to radio stations: "Acceleration Zone FM, All Rock, All Day" or "Windshadow FM, your source for light jazz, new age, and music for meditation."

Once past all that sleepy public radio windshadow business, we were finally sailing in classic trade winds! Easterly breeze, a good 12 – 15 knots, sunny blue skies with white puffy clouds. Our engine was running beautifully. *Tenacity* was sailing along proudly and strong. Our tanks were clean and filled with new clean diesel. Our lockers, nets and fridge topped off with fresh groceries. We were a happy crew on our way to Antigua!

MOTO GAZETTE
Middle Of The Ocean Gazette

Jan 6, 2013

<u>Headline News</u>

Bad Fuel Sold at Fuel Dock, in Las Palmas, Gran Canaria

Many of the yachts participating in this year's annual ARC regatta (Atlantic Rally for Cruisers), as well as many of recreational yachts also heading out from Las Palmas for the route crossing the Atlantic Ocean to ports Westbound, were caught off guard later when discovered their fuel tanks had been contaminated with water, sludge, bacteria, and a host of bad things that can possibly run havoc to a boat's diesel engine. Several of these boats suffered serious problems, such as fuel pumps breaking down, while others battled with clogged filters, dirty injectors and hours spent bleeding while hundreds of miles offshore. "This is really a shame that this fuel came from such a reputable place!" says American sailor Cindy Fletcher Holden, who with her Husband Robert, and Two Most Wonderful Crew Members John and Karen, had to detour to the island of Sao Vincente, in Cape Verde for repairs. Fortunately the city of Mindelo has Kai Brossmann, who owns the marina there and was able to get them back and running quickly, but not without spending a large amount of money!

Boats in the future should inquire as to when the last time the diesel tanks had been cleaned.

Huge Party Planned aboard Yacht *Tenacity* in the Atlantic Ocean

The crew of American sailing yacht, "*Tenacity*," is planning to host what could be the party of the year when they reach the half way point of their crossing, as little as three days from now. Crew members first mate Cindy Fletcher Holden and most Wonderful Crew Member Karen Lorenz are dutifully working on an extensive guest list which as of now includes the captain Robert

Holden and other Most Wonderful Crew Member John Prehn. Also included are ship's cats Perkins aka "Princess" and Dabola aka "Hisser," along with a nice family of dolphins that stop by on a regular basis, some flying fish, King Neptune and Keith Richards. Party entertainment will include a bunch of food already on board, three beers, Fanta Zero diet soda, some silly hats and maybe a cake.

American Sign Artist Collects Colors of the Ocean

American sign shop owner and Most Wonderful Crew Member aboard sailing yacht *Tenacity*, John Prehn, has successfully, using his Pantone Color matching app on his I phone, determined each and every color and it's Pantone corresponding color number surrounding the boat, including water, wave troughs, wave crests, sky, clouds, the boat's wake, deck, dodger, bimini, as well as the crew and the cats. "Aiming my phone at the one cat, Dabola, causes him to hiss and swat" says Prehn. "This job is more dangerous than I anticipated." *Tenacity* is owned by sail maker Robert Holden and his wife Cindy Fletcher Holden, who is also an artist, and joining Prehn as Most Wonderful Crew Member is Karen Lorenz, also an artist. "Only on a boat full of artists would something like this take place," says Fletcher Holden. "I'm just really glad we now know the proper colors."

A few days into the crossing, Karen knocked on our cabin top and said she had no steering. It was dawn. Robert got up and set the sails to hove to. We all got up. A bolt holding the tiller in place had broken. And to our surprise, we did not have a spare that was the exact same size. After some head scratching Robert actually turned the broken bolt around and used it that way. It worked. We decided to go into "Gentle Steering Mode" and try not to muscle the helm. Meanwhile, we searched the boat , like a scavenger hunt, for another bolt that would work. We found eight bolts that looked to be the same size, holding the compass binnacle down to the cockpit floor.

In a pinch, we could "borrow" one of those.

While Robert and John were inspecting the broken tiller, John noticed our still annoying stuffing box leak. This was still only a tiny trickle. It would allow water to puddle up under the bunk, and water down there isn't a good thing. Eventually it would spill out into the bilge and get pumped out. Robert explained how we had been searching for a right size wrench to tighten it the whole time we were cruising. And that we even hauled out for an out of the water inspection. At this point, John and Robert decided to just make their own wrench. I was on watch, steering happily once again, when Karen came out and announced we should have an art exhibit out there, in the ocean. Robert and John's masterful jury rigged concoction of towel rods, old tools, hose clamps and wire ties should be the featured art. I took a look and couldn't have agreed more. They came up with this makeshift wrench that they clamped onto the rudder post, turned it, and it worked! The trickle reduced to just a wet spot. We didn't have the art show however because no one responded to our invitations. Probably due to the fact we didn't send any out. But the leak stopped. And the homemade wrench was very cool.

Besides the steering bolt breaking, the whole trip was uneventful. Having Karen along made it special because it was her first time sailing across the ocean. We enjoyed her enthusiasm. We dined on more good meals every night. Karen became "Lunch Meister" and made all kinds of midday meals. We held two hour shifts and the whole watch system was easier this way. We had big wind, light wind, no wind, big waves, flat calm and absolutely wickedly stunning sunsets. These sunsets beat the ones we had on the way west. They deserved applause. All the wind was easterly. We did have swells from the north causing some side to side motion but we just dealt with it. The cats also dealt with it. Dabola does not like being in the ocean and hissed and swatted at anyone who walked by him, as if he were scolding us for putting him in this situation. Perkins actually seemed to like the trip. She loved Karen and John.

We saw lots of dolphins. One day, we saw some water splashing a few hundred feet away. Then we saw a large pod of little dolphins turn and race towards us. It was a huge pod with many dolphins! It looked like they were galloping! We laughed and squealed and loved having them join us for quite a long time! This was our biggest dolphin group of the trip! We also had a some birds join us in the beginning for a rest to wherever it was they were going.

Blog: Some Bickering Among Friends

Jan 8 2013
32:41.30N 16:54.00W

They are beyond exhaustion. Their legs haven't felt solid ground in nearly a week and they still have over 1400 miles to go before they reach land. Their arms are spent from holding course, even though it's all down wind. And they are starting to bicker over the smallest things. Who sits where, who steers better, who chooses which place for rest.

That is the life of three young white egrets, who have flown, or got flown, way off shore and chose our boat for refuge.

As they headed down to land on the boat, they fought, and steered each other off, while snapping at each other's heads. No doubt a pecking order in their world. Once safely perched on our dinghy davits, they held on tight with their strong little reptilian feet, pointed their white fuzzy heads into the wind, and at last, closed their eyes.

We wanted them to stay. We discussed what kind of options we had for feeding them. What do egrets eat? Little fish, stuff like this? They must need fresh water. We devised a plan to take some wet cat food (a brand our picky cats won't eat) and mix it with water and put in a bowl. But by the time our plan came to some order, our new friends took off.

Now I will worry and keep a look out for them. At least we provided a good nap!!!

MOTO GAZETTE
Middle Of The Ocean Gazette

January 11, 2013

Headline News

Seas Subside as American Yacht Enters Atlantic Demerara Abyssal Region

An American yacht "*Tenacity*" continues its journey across the Atlantic Ocean, from Cape Verde Islands to Antigua in the Lesser Antilles. The winds that were a solid 15 – 25 knots since the first day out, faded to nothing and the skipper, Robert Holden decided to motor until at least the winds return. The yacht is situated right past the half way point in an area known as the "Demerara Abyssal" to those who spend enough time looking at the chart and notice the odd names given to these oceanographic regions, which also include "Research Ridge" and "Vema Fracture Zone" (also a good name for a Rock Band).

After 9 days of healthy downwind to broad reach sailing, the crew of *Tenacity* take to some lounging, sunbathing, sun avoiding, napping, eating and basically enjoying a little break from the frolicking rock and roll motion that has not stopped since the first moment they left Cape Verde. In spite of the pleasant moment, the crew also hopes the winds return, so they can once again return to sailing, and therefore save fuel.

Besides considering fuel, *Tenacity's* crew has started some serious rationing of certain ship's items such as onions (only 7 left) Coca Colas (now for "Medicinal Use Only"), water (always frugal here) and Time spent opening the refrigerator. Still, this boat is considered a "Good Fooder" and crew members First Mate Cindy Fletcher "Extreme Cook" Holden, and Most Wonderful Crew Member Karen "Lunch Meister" Lorenz, will continue to create and expand the possibilities of ocean cuisine.

Business News

Tenacity Sea Products To Expand Beyond EverDamp

EverDamp, a well known and much loved part of sea life from Tenacity Sea Products, joined recently by "AllSalt," "InstaWet," "ShurSatch," and "RopeSkweek," now offers a variety of insurance policies, known as "EverSafe," and financial services known as "EverBroke." Also, crew members Cindy Fletcher Holden and Karen Lorenz are currently designing clothing and accessories, which will be called EverWear and will include the WrapAround Table Cloth, Paper Towel Sun Guard and Living Cat Scarf. EverWear will be holding its first Fashion show later this Spring.

EverDamp recently launched its first World Promotion Tour, and hopes to continue to expand into more exciting products and services!!

We ticked off the days on our chart. We had one small squall during my watch, during which I put on my Helly Hansen gear and recited my "Ode to Helly Hansen" while the rest of the crew stayed below and clapped.

Besides that little squall, and a few days of no wind, we had great weather. It was downwind sailing all the way. We'd sail wing on wing, with the jib on one side, held with a pole, and main on the other, no mizzen.

CHAPTER 44

Charlie

As we got closer to Antigua, our GPS estimated the time of arrival. As we got even closer, it had us arriving in the middle of the night of Jan 19. We didn't want to arrive in the dark. For our last night, we decided to hove to, relax, have a nice dinner, all get some sleep, and sail into Antigua in the morning light. Right after dinner (we named the meal "Hove To Chicken" which was creamy chicken and olives over pasta, seasoned with garlic, Spanish paprika and a bit of lemon) we spotted what looked like a large dark dolphin coming towards us from behind. As it got closer, we saw that it was far too big to be a dolphin. It was a whale! A big black dolphin shaped whale. Maybe a pilot whale? He swam right up to us, under the boat, and then turned over showing us his white belly. We named him Charlie, and, well, Charlie was enormous. He flipped back over and circled the boat, and flipped over again on his back. We were nervous. Charlie was huge. As big as the boat! We did not know what it was that Charlie wanted from us. We asked him nicely to not bash our boat. After about 30 minutes Charlie, maybe bored, swam away. Whew! As soon as Charlie was out of sight, we had a communal forehead slap when we realized no one had taken a photo.

After a good night's sleep spent hoved to, we adjusted our sails and continued west and not long after sunrise, saw the green island of Antigua rising up out of the horizon.

Antigua! Landfall! We sailed around the south side and entered English Harbor. It was a bright sunny day and the harbor was protected from the wind. We slipped quietly past a beach and a crowded anchorage to our right, and a boatyard tucked up in a lot of mangroves. We passed a classy marina to our left that berthed megayachts longer than city blocks. We slowly motored into a sheltered creek and dropped the anchor. We sailed across the ocean. Again.

Blog: Antigua

Jan 20, 2013
17:00.33N 61:45.56W

17 days across! Only 3 days of doldrums! The rest was all classic trade winds conditions! We had a splendid crossing! Terrific sunsets, delicious meals, resting egrets, little squalls, big waves, not so big waves, blue skies, white puffy clouds, cool nights, good books, good company, flying fish, galloping dolphins and a curious whale!

Now we take a break, gather up some fresh water, fuel and sleep, let our crew stretch their legs, and in a few days we will head to St. Thomas, and then up north to home!

We were back on the western side of the Atlantic now. We had sailed across the ocean twice. A big deal for us. Not a big deal for many sailors. A lot of the fellow cruisers we had met had a whole lot more sea miles under their hulls! Some had circled the globe several times. To some, crossing the Atlantic was merely another way to spend November or December. In fact, our friend Tony who we met back at the Tagus Boatyard, had crossed back and forth again since we met him. And he was by himself! He's the one who should be writing a book! But for us, in spite of what others had done, this was huge. We stuck with our dream and did it! We still had a long way to go to get home, but the big oceans were crossed.

CHAPTER 44

Caribbean

Arriving in Antigua on Jan 20 gave us a little more than two months to get back to Annapolis in time for "Spring Rush." Robert's employer said if we got back by mid April, there could be a very good chance he could get his same job back. We stayed in touch with them. Although we flirted with visions of opening our own canvas / sail loft, we both liked the idea of getting our feet back on financial ground with the ease of Robert's same position. Maybe we would open our own loft later, but for now we were hoping for a return to Robert's job. I had kept in touch with Annapolis people and had a few jobs lined up. One of them was an indoor wall mural, in a private home in Jacksonville, Florida, where we planned to stop anyway to visit family. All of this meant that we didn't have the luxury of time to really see the Caribbean Islands, but we still were able to enjoy some.

Back in September we contacted a friend, Sharee, who lives in St. Thomas, and asked her to join us for some of the Caribbean sailing. She suggested meeting in Antigua, and then work our way back to her home island. Sharee was going to Antigua anyway and told us it was an easy place to fly out of for Karen and John's return trip. After a few great days enjoying sunny Antigua, Karen and John took a taxi to the airport (knowing it was cold and snowing back in Annapolis!) It was sad to see them go. Robert and I sat on a little stone wall in silence watching the taxi pull away. Then Sharee joined us a couple days later. She sort of became an "unofficial Tour Guide" of a few of her favorite places

We also had been in contact with a friend from Annapolis, Chris Judy, who had interest in getting some ocean miles for a captain's license. We knew Chris from ice skating, and we knew he was a sailor as well. After a few e-mails and phone calls, we agreed on St. Barthelemy, more often referred do as St. Barts, as meeting spot with Chris and he made flight arrangements. Now we had logistics and schedules!

With Sharee, we sailed to the islands of Nevis and St. Kitts (same country), spent a few nights there, before sailing to St. Barts. The formalities took time. The officers were all very formal. We had read in our guide, that, ESPECIALLY in the Caribbean, it makes a difference what you wear when you check in. If you show up looking like a beach bum, baggy shorts and loose tank tops, they might not treat you so nice, since they are wearing hot dark suits and working in hot conditions. Robert always wore a nice shirt, and dress shorts and a belt and was treated with respect. I often wore running clothes, with which I broke the ice by asking for good running routes. This brought smiles and had officials giving us road maps and showing the best places for running. But showing our cats' Spanish passports was proving to be golden. We showed the St. Kitts officer our Spanish Cat passports, and he smiled broadly and stamped them! Wow! However the stamp said the cats could not seek gainful employment in St. Kitts.

Sharee is a seasoned sailor and a charter boat captain, so she knew her way around boats. I think our boat was slower than the big yachts she was used to. She showed us around a bit in Antigua and St. Kitts, and introduced us to a few folks she knew. Chris is a marine biologist, and a competent sailor, but has never sailed offshore. When he met us in St. Barts, he was grinning ear to ear with excitement about crewing on *Tenacity*. We decided to spend at least a day in St. Barts once Chris arrived before heading to St. Thomas.

At first, we were turned off by St. Barts. It's quite ritzy and expensive, we felt like we didn't belong there. Movie stars hang out there. Mega yachts even bigger than the ones in Antigua line the main sea wall of the harbor. The fenders on these boats are bigger than *Tenacity*! If any of these megayachts were in the US, the bow would have a different zip code than the stern. These are not cruise ships, they are privately owned yachts.

We heard rumors that the cheeseburgers sold at the "Cheeseburgers In Paradise Cafe" (made famous by Jimmy Buffet) were over $20. We saw cotton t-shirts for $100. We saw a white lacy swim suit cover-up for over $1000. In one store's front window a hammock was for sale for $37,000. This is not a typo. A HAMMOCK! For Thirty Seven THOUSAND Dollars! Here's the thing, the other islands all charge a lot of money to enter, (well over $100 a pop) and THEN they charge MORE money to exit! (THESE people are the pirates of the Caribbean!) Here in Movie Star Land/St. Barts, the charge was just $15. For the whole group of us. Done. Once I did the math, I liked the place.

After a day of R & R exploring beaches and gift shops, we sailed to St. Thomas. It was an easy 120 mile trip under a starry night and within sight of approximately one million cruise ships. When we were in spitting distance of Amalie harbor we saw a pretty feisty squall coming our way from behind. Our sails came down in time and we got to the anchorage and anchored safely before noon.

Checking in at customs was free here but still took quite a long time. The customs agent lady was not in a good mood. Some bad thing was ruining her day. I took out the heavy arsenal, the Cat Passports. We gave her the pile of passports, and when she got to the feline visas she was a bit confused. "What is this?" she asked. "Those are our cats' papers" I said. "A vet in Spain gave us passports" and just like that, we had her smiling, talking, and telling us her own cat stories.

Sharee was now in her stomping ground. Her neighbor Tom met us with her car and for the next few days, she took us around the island to the big grocery stores so we could load up the final stretch. Earlier, our engine would have a hard time starting and it was clearly in the ignition switch. If it didn't start right away, Robert would take off the wooden panel and start it from inside. For years it was ever so slightly fickle, and then recently it went from fickle, to annoying. Just a few days before we arrived in St. Thomas, it went to from annoying to possibly dangerous. Sharee had a car and knew where all the marine stores were so we were in a good spot to get a new ignition switch. We needed to take out the old one. While the switch was sitting in the front seat of Sharee's car, Robert had run back to the anchorage to fetch some last thing. He noticed *Tenacity* was dragging! This was the ONLY time in all the years we've been anchoring that it dragged. Robert couldn't start the engine with out the switch! The wind had picked up along with heavy rain and the boat was dragging right toward another boat, that was unoccupied and, of course, very shiny and looked brand new. Robert was there with the dinghy and a neighbor saw the whole scene and rushed over to assist. With both dinghies they got the boats safely to a better spot and re-anchored. It turned out the flukes of the anchor had gotten hold of long green grass, and not the bottom. I was watching from Sharee's car and was horrified and felt helpless. I actually bolted to some folks getting in their dinghy and asked in a panic for a ride to my boat. They asked which boat. "That one!" I responded excitedly, "The one that's dragging through the harbor!" It was pouring down rain when they ran me out and by the time we got there, Robert and our neighbor had everything under control, and I was soaked. But the boats were all safe. Whew!

A couple of days later, we had a new switch for *Tenacity*, new sunglasses for Robert, a cruising guide to Puerto Rico, an island scarf for Chris's wife, a little ceramic turtle with St. Thomas engraved on the shell for me and a boat load of groceries. We were heading to Florida! But, there was a big "Norther", or cold front, about to blow through. We had talked to another cruiser about our route to Florida and he strongly suggested the Old Bahama Channel. We bought charts for this. Then as we talked to a few more seasoned sailors from this part of the sailing world, we were as strongly urged to NOT do the Old Bahama Channel on account of the big Norther coming through because on this route there weren't any options to get shelter in a blow. Out in the open Atlantic, a big wind is a big wind, and you just either sail through it or adjust your direction and sail with it. But here, there are shallow banks, choral reefs and Cuba. It's best to either hunker down or get way offshore when the winter north winds blow. Instead of the Old Bahama Channel, we decided to sail to San Juan, Puerto Rico and ride out the blow. We said our good byes to Sharee and Tom (Tom bought one of my paintings) and sailed the 20 miles first to Culebra, which is part of Puerto Rico, with the intention of spending one night there and then head to San Juan.

CHAPTER 45

Unexpected Jewell!

At the southern side of Culebra there is a harbor called Ensenada Honda, and it is quite protected. We had our anchor down before dark and planned on an early morning exit for the 50 mile sail to San Juan. Robert was just getting into relaxation mood when Chris and I tried to convince him to put the engine on the dinghy and go into the little town of Dewey. From the anchorage, it didn't look like much. Robert finally gave in and we went in for a "look see" before it got really dark. After about a minute ashore, we were charmed. After about ten minutes, we were convinced to stay where we were for the blow and not go to San Juan. Dewey is a sweet little village. If there was a traffic light, I don't remember it. There is a ferry landing and a funky hotel there, a few gift shops, two Mom and Pop groceries, a barber, a couple of cafes and a taco joint, called Zaco's Tacos (It's fun to say "Zaco's Tacos") and it was the one of the popular spots to be. We also saw some chickens and a horse hanging around by the side of the road. We soon learned that Culebra is where residents of San Juan go for their weekends. We decided to stay especially after we read in our new cruising guide to Puerto Rico, that San Juan harbor could be subject to dangerous swell in a North wind and a North wind was in the forecast. Ensenada Honda was a snug harbor with good holding and no swell.

We stayed a few days waiting out the Norther. We found internet access in one cafe and at a municipal library that consisted of two trailers joined by a wooden porch. There were as many books out on the porch as inside the cramped trailers. The porch had tables and chairs, and a bulletin board with announcements for a beach barbeque or a community clean up day. Dewey has a reputation of no crime, and it was apparent with all the stuff out on the porch. We looked at the weather web sites and saw that this blow would last at least two days, maybe three, and then we would get some nice weather before the next front hit. This meant looking at the charts for the next place to hunker down. We had a cruising guide to the Bahamas, but no good charts. However, the Bahamas were in our GPS. We did a little research online and continued to watch the weather. It was looking like either we needed to head to Dominican Republic, or The Turks and Caicos. Either one was fine by me.

CHAPTER 46

Turks, Caicos, Cakes and Tacos

We enjoyed Culebra immensely. We visited gorgeous Flamingo Beach, all sunny with a big surf, a small but fascinating museum, (we learned the history of the island which is a story in itself). We shopped in the grocery stores, and Chris went to the barber. We stopped in several shops and just loved the down home feel of the place. It was wonderfully dusty and hot. The horses and chickens continued to wander around and good Spanish music played in cafes and stores.

Then the weather cleared and we headed out. We decided to go to Provincial, on the island of Caicos. This gave us a better vantage point for our beeline to Florida. The weather looked really good after this next cold front. But we had nothing in the way of charts for Caicos. Our GPS chart plotter did not include these islands. We did have some information in the cruising guide, which really isn't a good way to navigate. Once under way we called the number in the cruising guide for a marina called South Side that had a good reputation for shelter in a frontal system. On the phone we met Bob, and gave him our exact location. He gave us way points, as well as advice on getting to his marina. He suggested to anchor off of French Quay for the night, giving us exact way points to where to drop the anchor, and then to enter his marina the next morning at high tide.

According to all the forecasts, the weather would change in the late afternoon of the day of our arrival at South Side. We arrived to the "anchorage" just before dark and it was very strange to look down and see sand in less than ten feet of water, and see open ocean all around. We couldn't see French Quay, it was just a bit too dark. It was so eerie and weird we decided to still hold watch during the night even though the anchor was down. In the morning we saw French Quay, which was barely a spit of land, mostly sand, with maybe the highest point being two feet above sea level! The water's color was an amazing turquoise blue and as clear as glass. We pulled up the anchor and headed to South Side marina in calm winds.

We ran out of depth just outside the marina entrance and had to drop anchor and wait for more tide to come up. Before noon we were at the dock. We quickly met all the folks who were there in the sheltered marina for the exact same reason as we were. Bob and his marina people invited us to a Happy Hour party up at Bob's house above the marina office. Then some of the boat folks invited us to another Happy Hour party at the marina gazebo. We had been at this marina for less than 30 minutes and our social cards were over booked. We visited with everyone. The next day, Chris offered to rent a car for the day to tour the island. Caicos has a reputation for great snorkeling and diving but once this front came, we were in no mood to get cold and wet! Instead we drove around the whole island, trying to relax driving on the left side of the road, and saw the whole island in one long really great day.

Blog: "Parrotfish Poop, Potcake Pooches, Unexplained Ordinances and Cakes and Tacos"

Feb 20 2013

21:44.19 N 72:15.47 W

Our once thoughtfully conceived plan to sail directly from St. Thomas to Florida via the Old Bahama channel was scrapped in favor sailing to Culebra, (part of Puerto Rice) then sail North through the Bahamas. The change of plan was due to several nasty cold fronts, otherwise known as "Northers," blowing through the area. We were soon convinced that the Old Bahama Channel may not be the most comfortable or safe way to go being as how it's February and these Northers tend to blow through often this time of year, and can be really nasty.

Culebra was a few hours away, and we anchored in Ensenada Honda, and originally hadn't planned to go ashore, but did. Once ashore we fell in love with the place!! Such a welcoming small town feel. Quite Spanish, laid back and full of character. There are lots of cruisers hanging out and a good mainland U S "ex Pat" population, even though it is a U S Territory. There are no big stores, just 2 small grocery stores, mom and pop style, a library, a barber shop, a bakery, a few gift shops, a dive shop near the ferry landing, a few small hotels, some funky restaurants, a gas dock, a marine hardware store, a church, many roosters, several cats and a few horses. Nothing new and out of place. But there is a well maintained brightly painted orange lift bridge over a tiny canal that apparently was built for two fishing boats. We never did get the full history of this bridge but we did enjoy it's unusual character.

We did visit Culebra's biggest tourist attraction, Flamenco Beach, and besides loving it's incredible beauty, we also fell in love with the dozens of cats who live there and are friendly with people. We also visited a great little museum and learned that The U S Navy used Culebra as a bomb testing area for many many years, causing so many locals to leave, and then later the locals revolted, and after much talking to the US Government, the Culebrensans got their island back and got the U S Navy to pull out and leave them alone!!!! But, we did see signs to watch your step due to "Unexploded Ordinances." Made the walk to another beach more of an adventure indeed.

We left Culebra planning to head to Mayaguana in the Bahamas, and hopefully arrive there before the next big Norther that was scheduled to arrive in a few days with a vengeance. But it was looking like we weren't going to make Mayaguana so we headed to the Turks and Caicos islands. This was a ballsy decision because we have no charts for the Turks and Caicos, and we discovered that our GPS does not have detailed info for this place either. All we have is a cruising guide that has very little visual info. So we contacted Bob Pratt at South Side Marina in the town of Providenciales, also known as Provo, on the island Caicos. Bob guided us in with specific way points and advice to anchor off of French Cay over night so we could arrive to South Side Marina in the daylight. Anchoring off of French Cay was very weird, we were surrounded by open ocean, but in 15 ft of water!! We could see the bottom in the moonlight!! And we could hear whales but not see them!!! We had a nice quiet evening but still held watches throughout the night.

In the morning we saw French Cay, and it is just a very low small strip of beach!!!

We then followed Bob's way points in and were tied up in a safe slip in plenty of time to meet Bob, check in with immigration, go for a walk, trade a few books, start laundry and meet the neighbors at a daily informal "Happy Hour" under the cabana.

We learned that pretty much all the other boats in the marina were doing the same thing we were, waiting out the bad weather, which came in later that day and stayed for 2 days. We rented a car and toured the island and even though it was chilly and cloudy, we found the island of Caicos beautiful and friendly.

We noticed that there are these dogs everywhere. EVERYWHERE, and that look sort of alike, same size, medium to large, similar shape, sort of shepherd like with down turned ears, many brown, some black and tan, some pets and most wild. short but thick hair, and sort of friendly and very street smart. Turns out these dogs are called "Potcake Dogs," a mixed breed dog that over many generations have become their own breed and are named potcake after a traditional island food that the locals would feed to the dogs. Now there is an overpopulation problem and the local government is beginning to deal with it. Many folks are trying to adopt them as pets. The few we met were very sweet and I think they would be awesome pets!

One thing we found fascinating about Caicos is it is made of Coral. Unlike all the other islands that we have been visiting, that erupted from the sea's volcanoes, the island of Caicos emerged as the sea receded away. It is low and scrubby, the water is brilliant turquoise and in some places as clear as a swimming pool! It is a wonderful island!!

The name Caicos means "String of Islands" and the neighboring island Turks, is named after a cactus flower that looks like the red Turkish hat called a Fez. I guess an island named "Fez" isn't as appealing.

BUT by FAR, the best bit of new info we learned about this place, is that for MILLIONS of years, parrot fish have been eating coral with their sharp teeth. Imagine, parrot fish, eating coral for millions of years. Lots of coral, lots of hungry parrot fish. Then, the parrot fish poop out the coral, and it comes out like sand. So for millions of years, this is what has made up the sandy beaches of the island of Caicos. The sand that we've been walking on is really FISH POOP!!! Beaches made of million year old fish poop. Which is........

Better than walking on Potcake Pooch Poop!!

Once the cold front blew through, we headed out, and this time it looked like the weather would be perfect. And it was. It took us 4 days to sail to Ft.Lauderdale. Only one night the wind was strong enough to reef and I was exhausted from steering, but it was a good kind of tired. Chris was surprised at how consistently good the food was the whole time (I'm not surprised) and he proved to be wonderful crew. He was having such a good time his enthusiasm spilled over to us. It was a giddy four days of great sailing, sunsets, dinners and stories shared. Crossing the Gulf Stream down here was uneventful, although it could have been sloppy. We were lucky.

CHAPTER 47

Back In The USA

There we were! Back in the Continental U S A. First time since 2011! We entered Ft. Lauderdale inlet on a bright sunny afternoon with millions of boaters of every conceivable size among us. Tiny boats, jet skies, runabouts, ski boats, sport fishing boats, sailboats, big yachts and cruise ships. We looked up at one gigantic cruise ship just leaving the inlet and I yelled to the tiny people WAY up on the top deck, "WE JUST SAILED HERE ALL THE WAY FROM SPAIN." I don't know if they heard it but they all waved!

Chris made arrangements to fly home to the still snowy Annapolis, but not before spending a couple more days with us and soaking up the warm Florida sun and funky Ft. Lauderdale beach. The morning after a very tasty dinner out, we bid him farewell, and then it was the two of us, inside the waterway, for the final stretch home to Annapolis.

We had family, friends and a job to do on the way so we decided to stay inside the Intracoastal Waterway, also known as the ICW, the whole way home. The day after Chris left, another cold front swept through, this one packed with one long day of soaking heavy rain, and then on the other side of the front, it was cold. We had nights down to freezing and days inching their way up to maybe 50 degrees. We plodded along. Sometimes wrapped in full winter coats, scarves, hats and gloves. The winds were strong and stayed from the north so it was always right in our faces. At night we'd stop and anchor and crank up our ESPAR diesel heater. I'd cook a hot dinner and we'd curl up and watch a movie. Some say this is Yachting at its finest.

Blog: Follow The Magenta Line

March 1 2013

Once we entered the inlet at Ft. Lauderdale, we were officially in the Atlantic Intracoastal Waterway, also known as the AICW, and the ICW, and the "Ditch." It's a 1090 mile waterway that runs from Norfolk to Miami. Some of it follows natural waterways, such as rivers, bays and sounds, and much of it follows man made cuts, through land or between bodies of water. Parts of it goes through big cities like Miami, Ft. Lauderdale, Charleston, and Norfolk, and other parts go through smaller towns, like Beaufort and Beaufort, (pronounced BYOO fort and BOWfort) in South Carolina and North Carolina respectively. Many parts wind through marsh land with no civilization for many many miles, surrounded by grasses, creeks, swamps and some trees. More of the waterway goes through areas with big houses, mansions, ostentatious homes that scream money, cottages, shacks, trailers, even a tent now and then. Some parts pass marinas, resorts, restaurants, many wildlife reserve parks and an occasional rotting dock with no logical meaning.

The stretch from Ft. Lauderdale up to Ft. Pierce took us through dozens of bascule bridges that we had to call on VHF channel 9 to open. There is an expected courtesy when talking to bridge tenders. They like it when you know the exact name of the bridge, or they may not respond! Our chart plotter does not have the names, so I got into the habit of asking each bridge tender the name of the next bridge North bound so I would be ready. Some open on request, others only on half hour increments, which can be interesting if you have to hang around and wait with a swift current in a tight spot. But the most interesting thing I noticed during the whole bridge episode, was the chatter on channel 8 sounded more like the old CB radios in cars on the New Jersey Turnpike. Many people in the Ft. Lauderdale area have New York and New Jersey accents!

Much of the ICW is very shallow. The currents south of North Carolina can be wicked strong. 3 —4 knots at times! Especially in the man made cuts that connect tidal rivers, bays, and sounds. Our schedule has depended largely on the timing of the tides. There are a few stretches that we cannot get through except on a mid rising tide. Even here we get depths as shallow as 6 feet. If we were to go aground on an outgoing tide, it could cost us dearly. Some of these areas have 9 ft tides. So we need to be very aware!!

Steering along the ICW is more work than in the middle of the Ocean, not physically but mentally. You can't let go of the wheel even to scratch your nose or the current might shove the boat sideways, possibly into a shallow bank in some of the super skinny parts, or worse, a bridge. And then there are so many numbers to look at, the depth sounder, the boat speed, the wind speed, the marker numbers, the water temp, the oil pressure, the fridge temp. Sometimes, I'll look at the boat speed, which may get down to 4.5 if going against the current and I think "Oh no, it's getting shallow!" So many numbers.

The imagery is outstanding! Brilliant golden green grasses, tall skinny palm trees, old gnarly trees with hanging moss, funky trunks at the water's edge, tall pines and some beaches. Along with charming villages, old fishing boats, sparkly cities and manicured parks. The wildlife is spectacular! Lots of dolphins! We also saw a manatee, a stingray, a few turtles, lots of cormorants, herons, egrets and pelicans. I especially love the snowy egrets and how they have white feathery tops on their heads that they can raise and lower at will. I would love to be able to do that with my hair! Like when I meet someone new, I could make my hair go straight up, and then back down. I also love the pelicans! They are huge birds! And they look like they haven't changed much since dinosaur days. These birds often fly inches above the water with their wings spread wide, and sometimes they fly in formation with other pelicans, like the Blue Angel pilots. Pelicans may think they are intimidating due to their size, and long strong beaks, but they have fluffy yellow fuzz on the tops of the heads that just make you want to go up and scratch their furry heads! I would love to have a pet pelican. I'd name him "Mr. P", and he would follow me around where ever I go. Yeah right.

Traveling up the ICW has been much different than our European part of the adventure! For one thing the locals all speak English! We can read the signs! And we see land the whole time, sometimes almost too close for comfort. But as it has been during the whole time, the people have been friendly. They really light up when we mention that we are returning from a sail to Europe! And they light up more when we clearly are as excited about being in whatever town we are in as we were in every place in Europe!! SO we will continue up the ICW and into the Chesapeake as we trek on home! Me, Robert, Perkins, Dabola, and Mr P. Well, maybe not the pelican.

We stopped in Jacksonville where I had a potential wall mural. The customers, Mike and Heather, were from Annapolis and I had done an extensive mural project in their house there years ago. Now they were in Florida. Earlier this year, we got together again via e-mail and made a plan to have me do something in their new house in Ponte Vedre beach, just outside of Jacksonville Beach. We found a spot to anchor as close as possible to their house. Mike came and picked me up and took me to see the room. What I had thought was going to be a small one day job turned out to be a three wall mural that took two weeks to complete! I absolutely loved doing the job and the pay was great! Heather or Mike would come and get me in the morning and bring me back in the evening. It was still cold. We would cozy up in our cabin at night, cook and watch movies. Then we got up early and I would go to work on the mural.

Meanwhile, Robert did a whole host of chores on the boat and one day discovered a hydraulic fluid leak in our steering system. He ordered a new pump, using Mike and Heather's house as a shipping address. When the mural was all done, we decided to splurge and go into a marina just a couple of miles away, and install the pump with the possible assistance of dock power, as well as visit with Robert's aging mother who wouldn't have been able to visit by dinghy. We also planned on a dinner out celebrating the new mural with Mike and Heather, who by this time were thoroughly bonded to both of us.

We hoped that topping off the fluid in the steering pump would get us to the marina but the steering did not work as soon as we were underway. Good thing this all happened in a safe place. AND good thing Robert redesigned the emergency steering way back in Norfolk, before we ever left, because now we had to test it. We only had a couple of miles to go, and thankfully there was no wind at all (the forecast was for over 20 knots). We only had to deal with some current and going under one bridge. I stayed at the throttle and gear shift, (all working just fine) and Robert stood on the emergency tiller, using his feet to steer. He stood up and he could easily see outside. We worked as a team. I called the marina and let them know we were coming in and that we were slightly handicapped and would need assistance docking. Fine, they said. We made the 90 degree turn off the main channel and followed the marina's private markers to the dock. As we got closer, I approached the dock as I normally would but instead of turning the wheel, I would say left or right to Robert, and used the gear shift and throttle as I normally do. We made a perfect landing. The guys at the dock were standing around with their hands in their pockets. They later said they had no idea we didn't have normal steering. They remembered me telling them we would be handicapped but figured we fixed it. There you go! Sure had them fooled.

CHAPTER 48

The Final Leg

Visits finished, hydraulic pump installed, big mural job done, celebration dinner enjoyed, we kept on going north. We stopped every night and visited several more friends on the way up. We went though winding rivers, skinny canals, and big bays. We encountered wicked currents and stiff headwinds. We successfully missed hidden rock piles, and hunkered down twice due to horrible weather. We did run aground once, oops, make that twice, in the channel, and just waited until the tide came up. We found all the grocery stores and became reacquainted with U.S. food and prices. We bought chocolate and Parmesan cheese. We reactivated our cell phones and called everyone in our contact lists. I even called my mechanic Fred to get my old Jeep up and running. We called around and decided to go back to the same marina we were in before. We finally got to Norfolk and entered the Chesapeake Bay. We stopped in Solomon's, MD, just 80 miles from Annapolis to wash the boat and get it all spiffed up. Another cold front was about to hit and this one was huge, bringing with it several tornadoes and 60 mph winds. Dandy! Another tornado. We survived this storm at the dock, and then the next day pushed our way up the Bay into 35 knot winds out of the north and 35 degree temperatures! Kind of miserably cold but it was sunny! What a way to come home!

We spent one final night a few miles south of Annapolis, to just let it settle in our heads that we about to be back. We called everyone who might show up and said we'd be at the dock around 3:00 PM the next day, a Sunday afternoon. In the morning, we hung our signal flags so they would read "TENACITY ROCKS" and then we hung all the flags from every port we visited. The boat looked magnificent. All colorful and festive! The boat looked happy. I think it even purred. We pulled the anchor up and headed back to

Annapolis. Right at 3:00 we turned the corner of Back Creek, our home creek, and motored into our new slip. A dock full of family and friends were there with bags of champagne, cups, and lots of hugs. We were home!

Epilogue

Tenacity is back in the same slip we had before the big adventure. The cabin is still ready for offshore. Things are are still secured inside. The jack lines still run along the deck.

Robert is back at the sail loft and I am busy painting boat names and murals.

We are back on the ice with our ice dancing skating faster and better than before, although it took a while to get our ice legs back.

We had to buy new (used) cars but we bought pretty much bought the same kinds of cars as before, a big van for Robert which also serves as storage, and a newer Jeep Cherokee (same color as before) for me which serves as a big paint box on wheels. So in some ways it's the same life we had before the trip.

But it's not. Nearly everyday, something sparks a memory from the trip. Sometimes a simple thing like a song on the radio will remind me of sitting in the office at the Oeiras Marina, or a sound will remind us of the quirky ambulance sirens in Las Palmas, and many many more. I often close my eyes and try to remember the feeling of being in the ocean at night under the stars. I even try to relive that first storm! Every now and then I find a little note that someone wrote with a Portuguese word on it and what it means, or a receipt from a Spanish store, or a ticket from the Lisbon subway. And of course we have thousands of photos that we never get tired of viewing. The memories will stay, hopefully forever.

Crossing an ocean does something to you. I look at our passage chart (hung on my studio wall) and realize that we sailed across the ocean. And back. It's a cool feeling. It sort of gives you a stronger spine.

People often ask what was our favorite place. This is a hard question. The Azores had that special magic but we loved every place, town, village, city, marina, harbor, store and cafe. But sometimes, when I really think about it, I loved the ocean the most. The stars, the waves, the white puffy clouds and epic sunsets, and *Tenacity* sailing across it with what seemed like real joy. We are two of those people that believe boats have souls. After this trip, we are convinced.

Thanks to social media, we still keep in touch with our new friends! Our friend Tony even made it to Annapolis and we've been hanging out with him here. We talk to Alan on the phone occasionally and of course Karen and John are here in the same town. In fact, Karen rents my front part of the studio so we get to visit frequently.

I've been writing articles for sailing magazines. Remember Patrick Ramano? The thief who got my wallet? I sent a magazine with an article I wrote about dancing the tango in the police station in Mindelo to the police! I may never know if Mr Ramano himself sees the magazine but the police will, and I hope it will bring a smile to their faces!

And now I have this book! I could not have done it without the help of my sister Jackie and my friend Dennis! Of course I wouldn't have this book without Robert's excellent seamanship and captain skills. It could have been "Tales of Disaster" but it was instead a great, fun, life changing ride. Maybe we'll do it again! But meanwhile, we are back, *Tenacity* looks as beautiful as ever and everything is in good working order. We are enjoying gainful employment. The cats are happy that the big waves are now gone, far away and "out there". Life is good.

Tenacity Specs

Dillon Offshore 47
custom Bruce Roberts design

year.....1986
length........47'
width.....13.5'
gross tonnage.........22
displacement.....32000lbs
draft....5' 10"
Bottom configuration.....modified fin keel with skeg supported rudder
steering....hydraulic
Auto pilot.....Wagner, electric
rig......ketch , aluminum masts and booms
engine.......Perkins 4.154 diesel four cylinder 52 hp
hull........fiberglass and strong as a battleship
water capacity..........550 gallons
fuel capacity...........125 gallons
cooking....three burner LPG stove/oven
bunks.......... v berths in forward cabin. Queen bunk in aft cabin
electronic navigation........Garmin 4208 GPS/chart plotter
communication..........Icom M 45 VHF radio, Iridium Sat phone
solar panels.......Ferris Marine, 2
wind generator......Air Breeze, mizzen mounted
refrigeration/freezer.....Frigoboat keel cooler
batteries........6 Trojan golf cart
sails.........made by Robert
furling system....Furlex
anchor....44lb bruce
cats....domestic short hair
entertainment..........20" Toshiba flat screen TV with Sony DVR/VHS video
system, JVC AM/FM CD stereo, our imagination, and the cats
books........probably well over a hundred
storage capacity....Lots!

About the author

Cindy Fletcher Holden is a freelance artist living in Annapolis MD. She specializes in hand lettering boats, wall murals and oil paintings on canvas. She started a biannual group art exhibition called Art Between The Creeks that has been going strong since 2003. Her murals are on several buildings throughout Annapolis as well as two in Portugal and one in Spain. Her paintings have been shown in several cities including "The New Millennium" group show in New York City at the Lindenburg Gallery.

She started boating as an infant and started handling power boats as a young girl. She started sailing at 16 and bought her own boat at 17, which she sailed down the Intracoastal Waterway soon after college. She married professional sailmaker Robert Holden in 1988 and learned more about sailing and racing, and crewed on many local race boats mainly on the foredeck.

When she isn't painting she could be found practicing ice dancing with Robert, or writing articles about cruising. Her articles has been published in Cruising Outpost magazine and Spinsheet magazine.

Several articles have been written about Cindy's art work as well as Robert and Cindy's travels in the Baltimore Sun, the Annapolis Capital, Spinsheet magazine, Severna Park Voice and Chesapeake Bay magazine. For more information visit the web site www.fletcherart.net.

Made in the USA
Middletown, DE
20 December 2014